*When Nations Disagree*

ARTHUR LARSON

# *When*

# *Nations Disagree*

A Handbook on Peace Through Law

LOUISIANA
STATE UNIVERSITY PRESS

OTHER BOOKS BY ARTHUR LARSON

*Cases and Materials on the Law of Corporations*
  (with R. S. Stevens)
*The Law of Workmen's Compensation*
*Know Your Social Security*
*A Republican Looks at His Party*
*What We Are For*

Copyright 1961 by
Louisiana State University Press
Library of Congress Catalogue Card Number: 61–15490
Manufactured in the United States of America by
Kingsport Press, Inc.

*To Lex and Anna*

# Table of Contents

*When Nations Disagree*

# The World Rule of Law Idea

𝖕𝖕𝖕𝖕𝖕𝖕𝖕𝖕𝖕𝖕𝖕𝖕𝖕𝖕𝖕𝖕𝖕𝖕𝖕𝖕𝖕𝖕

THE "WORLD RULE OF LAW" IDEA HAS THIS
primary objective: to strengthen the body, the machinery,
the acceptance, and the sanctions of international law so
that law will increasingly come to occupy the place in international affairs that it does in the domestic affairs of
civilized nations. For years people have been calling for a
positive plan for world peace. Everyone knows that past
efforts have been too often negative. Get rid of war. Get
rid of armaments. But we cannot just get rid of these
things and leave a vacuum. Something else must be put in
their place. What is that something? In the human
story, it has always been law.

This truth is dramatized every night on television as
we witness the endless retelling of the story of the Wild
West. We could not just eliminate the six-gun and leave
nothing in its place. Only with the advent of law, per-
sonified by sheriffs, marshalls, and courageous local courts
and citizens, could the rule of force be displaced. The
same lesson is taught by the story of how rule of law sup-

planted rule of force in England. The armies of the quarreling lords and barons were not dismantled one fine feudal day in a burst of peace-loving fervor. What happened was that the king's courts were created, gained acceptance, and proved their workability. Only then were the feudal armies abandoned, as the new and peaceful way of settling quarrels became established.

How do we go about creating a world rule of law? What are the component parts, the building blocks, of any system of legal order? How can we get down to the business of creating methodically these component parts on the international scale? There has been far too much remoteness and mystery surrounding this idea of world legal order. To many people the concept of world rule of law is a sort of beneficent but disembodied presence in the sky whose name is invoked in the hope that it will somehow descend and miraculously exorcise the demon of war. This is not the idea at all.

If we want to build a house, we identify the needed parts—foundation, walls, roof, doors and windows, plumbing and wiring, and so on—and we then make them and put them together. What, then, are the normal ingredients of a working system of law for the settlement of disputes? Let us review what we have, what we do not have, and what we will have to add or change to provide a world legal system worthy of the name.

There are four main ingredients in such a system:

1. A body of law that is accessible, up to date, and capable of deciding the disputes that cause tension in the world as it is today.

2. Machinery to apply that law—machinery which is

also accessible, up to date, and adapted to settling the kind of disputes that today's world produces.

3. Acceptance of that body and that machinery of law by the persons affected—and here we must remind ourselves that many of the people of the world do not regard present international law and tribunals as their law and their tribunals.

4. Compliance with the decisions of international tribunals once they are rendered.

This statement of the exact job to be done in building the rule of law on an international scale is stressed at the outset because the rather novel terms "world rule of law" and "world law" are sometimes given meanings that are either too narrow or too broad and vague.

Perhaps because of the lively dispute over the extent of the United States' acceptance of World Court jurisdiction there is danger of getting the impression that there is nothing more to world rule of law than the settlement of an occasional international legal dispute by the International Court of Justice. However, as the index to this book and the summary of components of the legal order will show, the actual decision of a case in court is only a small part of the total pattern of law on the international scene, just as it is on the domestic scene. Most people go through life without ever actually appearing in court as a plaintiff or defendant; yet everything we do is surrounded by the security, order, and peace created by the rule of law in domestic affairs.

On the other hand, if a concept of "world law" is given too diffuse a scope, it loses its distinctive power to set a clear line for practical action. Therefore the term is not used here to cover the whole range of possible actions to strengthen the United Nations and other international organizations in their legislative or executive capacities nor to encourage the many other important moves—political, diplomatic, economic, educational, and cultural—that have a part to play in building a peaceful world. The precise purpose here is to see how the resources of law can be directly brought to bear on the problem of preventing conflict and building peace.

By comparison with some of the other resources, such as the economic, informational, and scientific, the resources of law have been neglected in the efforts for peace that have been made since World War II. This is the more surprising when one remembers that law is one of the few such forces in the world that is widely understood and relatively unspoiled. Practically everyone in the world understands the concept of law. Indeed, as will be shown later, the degree of consensus among human beings on the fundamental principles of law is quite surprising. At the same time, practically everyone respects law. It is not one of those words that has been twisted out of its true meaning by propaganda, as has happened in the case of such words as "democracy." Nor has it been tainted by the mistrust felt by many people toward such forces as mass media, politics, and diplomacy.

But, it is sometimes asked, can law really be of help in the big disputes that threaten world peace? Are not the big disputes questions of politics and diplomacy?

It comes as something of a surprise to people who raise these questions to learn that most of the dangerous international disputes of our time have legal questions embedded in them. This is not to say that, in today's imperfect world, the nations of the world are in fact willing to settle these legal questions by legal means. The point is that these questions, by their inherent nature and quality, are of a kind which could be handled by legal methods—if the parties would agree to this method of handling.

The Suez dispute centered around the alleged breach of Egypt's agreement with the Universal Suez Canal Company and the Convention of Constantinople of 1888. It could have been appropriately submitted to an international tribunal, as was the nationalization of the Anglo-Iranian Oil Company, an event which also threatened to precipitate war in the Middle East.

The present Suez dispute, which takes the form of objections by Israel to Egypt's practice of blocking and searching Israel-bound shipping desiring to transit the Suez Canal, consists of a number of questions which are almost all legal in character.

Another justiciable dispute causing tension in the Middle East is the controversy on whether the Gulf of Aqaba and the Straits of Tiran are legally waters open to innocent passage by Israel-bound cargo.

The Berlin crisis involves several legal disputes. The principal legal questions concern rights of access under various agreements and under doctrines such as easement of necessity, and the Soviet claim of right to transfer its obligations under the Four-Power Pact to East Germany, as well as the legal effect of any such transfer attempt on destruction of Western rights of access and of Soviet obligations generally.

Claims of expropriations of private property and of interference with international investment, as in Cuba or Indonesia, are intrinsically susceptible of judicial determination.

Boundary disputes are generally by nature amenable to judicial settlement. The International Court has already handled several such disputes. The boundary dispute between China and India, which has all the potentialities of a major source of tension, is in this category.

Aerial incidents are amenable to International Court treatment, and a number of attempts to bring them into court have been made by the United States.

This brief listing, which is amplified in Chapter 16, is intended only as a preliminary indication that many of the disputes that are threatening world peace today are in whole or in part the kind of disputes that the International Court could help settle peaceably. Sometimes, of course, there are mixed questions of law and diplomacy in a controversy. For example, the Berlin question is a mixture of disputes over present rights under existing agreements, which are justiciable questions, and disputes over what changes should be made in any new regime that might be set up for Berlin and Germany, which questions are obviously political and diplomatic. But this does not mean that the judicial process would not make an important contribution. In such mixed controversies the judicial process could put to rest matters concerning existing legal rights and could forestall arbitrary one-sided action in disregard of present agreements and rights, such as is periodically threatened in the Berlin situation. The maintenance of peace and order through the application of law to existing rights in this way might also well encourage the settlement by peaceful means of related disputes involving demands for change. In a more general sense, the gradual strengthening of the judicial process in the world would serve to enhance the "habit of law" in international affairs as against impulsive and high-handed disregard of legal rights and procedures.

The true measure, then, of the contribution of the peace through law movement will be found not merely in the number of actual disputes settled in court but also in the general increase in respect for legal rights and procedures and in the general elevation of the standard of international conduct that would flow from the strengthening of the substance and machinery of international law.

# PART ONE

# *The Body of World Law*

🮖🮖🮖🮖🮖🮖🮖🮖🮖🮖🮖🮖🮖🮖🮖🮖🮖🮖🮖🮖🮖🮖🮖🮖🮖🮖

## ( 1 )

## Is There Such a Thing as International Law?

IT IS A FAVORITE GAMBIT OF SOME CYNICS TO
say that international law is not really law at all. Because
the whole subject seems so remote and mysterious to most
people, it is easy for this kind of suspicion to become
widespread.

It is difficult to think of international law as being
as real as the traffic laws that govern driving on a local
street. Yet, are there not traffic laws on the high seas?
It is just as important at sea as on land to know whether
you pass to the right or to the left. On the whole, traffic
laws of the sea are just as well obeyed as those on land—
indeed, probably better obeyed.

There are two main reasons why some people deny
that international law is real law. Both stem from a misconception of what is law itself.

The first reason is that there seems to be no legislative

body passing international statutes. We look about us on the domestic scene and see Congress, state legislatures, county and city bodies, all passing binding laws and ordinances. But we look in vain for their counterpart on the world scene.

The mistake is to suppose that legislation is the only, or even the primary, source of law. Most of the law we live by is not originally based on legislation at all.

Suppose your employee negligently pokes his shovel handle into my eye while he is shoveling snow for you. It would be accepted all around without question that you, as employer, are liable to me in damages for the act of the employee. Yet this did not come about by legislation. It came about because a single judge, Lord John Holt, sitting in a lower court in England in 1698, uttered the edict: the act of the servant is the act of the master. The phrase had a certain antiphonal lilt to it that produced a plausible and hypnotic effect. Moreover, it dealt with a real social problem, which was the normal inability of servants to pay for the damage they caused. And so it caught on and became the basis for employers' liability in countless highway and other accident cases.

Through thousands of such cases decided over the centuries there grew up what is called common law.

At the international level there has also grown up, without the assistance of a world legislature, a vast and varied collection of laws regulating everyday transactions. Among the sources of these rules are: customary international law, bilateral treaties, multilateral treaties, judicial decisions of international tribunals, arbitral awards, decisions of national or state courts on international law questions, diplomatic correspondence, regulations issued by international bodies including United Nations agencies, writings on international law by recognized authorities, and the general principles of law recognized by civilized nations.

The second reason the reality of international law is sometimes questioned is that there is no superpoliceman with a big club ready to hit anyone over the head who violates the law.

The important fact is that people and nations do comply with the rules of international law when authoritatively applied by qualified tribunals. True, they sometimes break them, just as people break domestic laws. Once in a while international gangsters will defy the entire legal system, just as domestic gangsters will sometimes set up an empire that operates outside the law. But generally, international decisions are as well observed as national.

In all the decisions of the Permanent Court of International Justice and the International Court of Justice there is only one case of disobedience. Among hundreds of arbitral decisions and thousands of rulings of various other tribunals there will be found no more than a small handful of instances in which the question of compliance has even arisen. The reason for this record will be discussed later in connection with the over-all subject of enforcement. At this point it is mentioned merely to dispel the common assumption that it is useless even to talk about a body of world law in the absence of a legislature and a superpolice force.

# (2)
# Marshaling Existing Law

THE TASK OF BRINGING THE BODY OF WORLD law up to the standard expected of a regular legal system divides itself into two parts: making existing law accessible; and going beyond to create a kind of law that will be usable by, and acceptable to, not just Western Christendom but all of the more than one hundred nations of the world.

As to accessibility, although many of the major treaties, decisions, and other sources are published and available, large amounts of international law are scattered, unpublished, and hard to reach.

Suppose Country A and Country B are having a dispute about their relative rights to use the waters of a river that flows through both countries. Country A contends that there is no international law on the subject. Also suppose that during the past century there have been two hundred instances in which countries with a similar dispute have disposed of their problem under international law, by treaty, by diplomatic letter, by arbitration awards, by judicial decisions of either national or international bodies, and by customary international law. Assume that in almost every case the parties had recognized a principle, say, that both countries have a right to an equitable share in the waters of the river. Theoretically, this should mean that there is in fact a rule of international law to that effect. But—and here is the catch—what good is that rule of international law to Country B if Country B cannot find and demonstrate all these evidences of international law, which may be scattered in the filing cabinets of foreign offices and in unpublished reports on the shelves of distant libraries?

So we face a stark axiom. Nonaccessible law is nonexistent law. Philosophers may debate whether there is really a sound when a tree crashes in a wilderness and the sound is not heard by any living creature. But lawyers know that, for all practical purposes, there is really no legal rule when the evidence of its existence cannot be found and therefore is never heard by any judge. The objective is clear enough: the materials and evidences of international law should be published, annotated, indexed, and cross-referenced to the same extent as domestic materials. But where is the Shepard's Citator of international law? the key-number system? the regional reporter system? the annotated statutes? the Federal Register? the L.R.A., the A.L.R., the C.J. and A.J. and W. & P. and U.S.C.A. and N.C.C.A.—not to mention the endless loose-leaf publications that keep lawyers poor, publishers prosperous, and secretaries frantic?

By contrast, in preparing cases under domestic law, we take it for granted that in a matter of hours we can find in any working law library all the cases decided since the seventeenth century in which a pawned diamond was stolen by the pawnbroker's servant or in which a drunken stableman was bitten by a cat. Since the domestic lawyer has access to such well-organized material, the development of domestic law can, to a considerable degree, be left to the initiative of litigants in individual cases. But on the international scene it is too much to expect of a lawyer, after he is confronted with a particular international law case, to comb the entire globe for evidences of customary international law, general principles of law recognized by civilized nations, and other sources of international law. If the job is to be done at all, it has to be done in advance by scholars, research centers, and professional associations.

This phase of the world rule of law job is deliberately mentioned first because it is perhaps the most mundane and unglamorous of all. Such a piece of work, which could keep dozens of scholars and lawyers busy for years, may seem a far cry from prophetic visions of a world that lives under law—and yet how can a world live under law until it can first find out what the law is?

Efforts in this direction have been made from time to time in the past, but the story has frequently ended in frustration or at best in only fragmentary achievement. John Bassett Moore's *International Adjudications* (1929) survived for only seven volumes. Herbert Arthur Smith's *Great Britain and the Law of the Nations* (1932) went to only two volumes. In the literature of international law one encounters everywhere the same refrain: The system urgently needs a definitive and regular reporting and digest system which is not dependent on the life or inspiration of a single individual. The International Law Commission of the United Nations published a report emphatically documenting this need, but more than ten years have passed and the all-out effort has still not been made. The Sixth (Legal) Committee of the United Nations has for some time had under discussion the publication of a Juridical Yearbook, but at this writing no action has emerged. Such a publication would help marshal another source of materials—the extensive periodical literature in many languages whose inaccessibility has been pointed out by such scholars as Maxwell Cohen. Here, then, is a task that could challenge the best talents and energies not only of the universities and foundations but also of international and national organizations, in a great cooperative effort to achieve this first essential of a world legal system.

It is an attractive analogy to say, as Wilfred Jenks does in his remarkable book entitled *The Common Law of Mankind* (1958), that we are now at a stage in the evolution of a common law in international relations comparable to the early stages of the common law in England. However, if this analogy is to work itself out, we must remember one thing: The nature of a common law system presupposes that decisions and other evidences of law are known and accessible.

Since a task of such magnitude must be spread over years, the best approach may be to begin with areas of law where accessibility of law would now have the most to contribute to relieving of tensions. A good example is the need to compile and annotate all the law bearing on international rivers, so that authoritative guidance will be at hand to aid in the settlement of the many festering disputes on rights in international waters.

This pressing need to make international law materials more accessible coincides with an exciting new development in methods of storing and handling legal information. Experiments in other fields, and some preliminary experiments in the legal field, indicate the practicality of reducing legal data to coded form so that it may be stored in electronic computers and retrieved at will. One is apt to think of computers as dealing largely with numbers, but there are various ways of translating nonnumerical concepts into numerical form, and once this has been done the concept and its relationship to other concepts can be stored on electronic tape just as books and digests can be stored in a library.

An interesting example of the use of this technique for nonnumerical data is the experiment that has been carried on for several years at Western Reserve University. The subject of the experiment has been metallurgy rather than law, but the same techniques could be adapted to law. The entire contents of all the journals of the American Metallurgical Society have been reduced to coded form and stored on tape. Members of the society have been invited to send in any questions they might have about where to find the results of past research and writing. For example, a member writes in and says: "I want to find all of the material available on the effects of water upon beryllium and beryllium compounds." The question is "programmed" by plugging in a number of elements in the question into the machine, a switch is thrown, and the machine begins to search its memory to find anything that has this particular combination of elements and relationships. To one side of the machine stands an automatic typewriter, which now and then suddenly comes to life and begins to type furiously. When the machine has run its course, one will find on a long sheet of paper the author's name, article, volume and page of every discussion of the effect of water on beryllium or beryllium compounds.

Somewhat similar experiments have been going on with legal data in case form in the United States Patent Office and in statute form at the Health Law Program of the University of Pittsburgh. There are various ways in which information can be coded. It can be coded according to numerical symbols for actual words, as in some of the legal experiments; or it can be coded according to concepts and relationships, as in the metallurgical experiment. The latter has the advantage of not being dependent on any particular language. The same numerical code can be used for English, Japanese, Russian, or any other language. For example, in the Western Reserve code book it became necessary to find a code number for the kind of vacuum tube known as a "peanut tube." It would obviously have confused the machine badly if the code for "peanut" and the code for "tube" had been used. The word code "peanut" would have sent the machine on a wild chase through the vegetable department, while the word code "tube" would have dragged in all sorts of pipes and conduits and soda straws. Accordingly, it became necessary to ask precisely what a vacuum tube is. Actually, it is a valve which controls the passage of electrons, and the "peanut" part of the designation is simply a picturesque way of denoting its small size and its peculiar shape which can be described in more accurate ways.

Since the field of international law naturally involves many languages, it is quite possible that the conceptual rather than the word-for-word approach would be necessary. In addition, there are other ways of storing information which might have a part to play. The Eastman Minicard machine puts four full pages of printing on a small film in a card about the size of a special delivery stamp, together with the necessary code symbols to bring it out on demand. There could be stored the entire texts of some legal sources, or at least adequate summaries and digests of cases, statutes, treaties, and the like. Even maps and drawings can be stored in this way.

The American Bar Association has an electronic data retrieval committee which issues a publication called *MULL*. This title, like many modern titles, appears to have been chosen with an eye to the connotations of its initials, with their atmosphere of pensive deliberation; but the initials do stand for actual words, "Modern Uses of Logic in Law." The committee, which never expected to have more than about fifty subscribers to the periodical, was astonished to find a demand for over five hundred subscriptions almost at once—an indication of the rapidly growing interest in this new method of handling legal materials. The difficulties and the amount of work to be done are enormous, but the rewards of success would be even greater, particularly in the international field.

There are two reasons why the application of this technique to international and foreign law is even more urgent and promising than its application to domestic law. One is that domestic law sources are already relatively well digested, indexed, and cross-referenced, while international law sources still have most of this work to be done. One cannot escape the feeling that, if the job is to be done now, it might as well be handled by the most up-to-date methods, and this means electronic storage and retrieval. The other reason is that this approach could go a long way toward surmounting language difficulties. In this connection it is relevant to call attention to the remarkable developments made in translating material from one language to another by electronic methods. One of the things that the electronic method does is to compel everyone to say exactly what he means. When an idea is reduced to numerical coded form, there is no room for slipshod meanings or hazy implications. An incidental benefit, then, may be to sweep much of the semantic fuzziness out of our communications and to make sure that, when we are dealing with people from other countries, the words used really mean what we think they do.

Of course, to do the entire job of electronic coding and storage of international law materials would be a task of fantastic proportions extending over many years and costing many millions of dollars. But a start could be made on particular areas where the returns might be relatively prompt. For example, the business community could well afford to finance the establishment of a clearinghouse which would reduce to coded form all the legal data bearing on problems of international investment. As matters now stand, with the laws of over a hundred independent nations to deal with, the desirable increase of private investment abroad is sometimes impeded by the sheer difficulty of finding out what the legal situation is.

Suppose an American, British, or German investor decides he would like to make a substantial private investment in some enterprise in Southeast Asia, Africa, or Latin America. Naturally he wants to know what he is getting into, so far as tax laws, corporation laws, labor laws, currency restrictions, and a host of other laws are concerned. A central clearinghouse of the kind here suggested could be so designed as to give him the information tailored to his particular needs. Under present methods the difficulties of getting answers to these legal questions are sometimes so formidable that, rather than take a chance, the investor throws up his hands and decides to invest his money closer to home. In view of the urgency of getting more private capital into underdeveloped countries, the setting up of such a clearinghouse would serve not only a practical business purpose but also an important function in raising economic standards throughout the world.

# (3)
# What Is World Law?

EVEN IF ALL EXISTING MATERIALS OF LAW were conveniently accessible, there remains the question: Is existing international law adequate to the task of keeping the peace in today's world?

It is not. We need a new concept of its purpose, its range, and its content. To signalize this changed concept, it is useful to have a new name. That is why the phrase "world law" is used here.

*New concept of purpose:* While classical international law had the purpose of regulating the affairs of nations generally in war, in peace, and in neutrality, world law stresses one purpose—to keep the peace.

*New concept of the range of world law:* It must become the thread that holds together the fabric of a universal legal order based on the free adherence of more than a hundred nations. International law in the traditional sense is associated with a system which was largely the handiwork of the nations of Western Christendom. Its sources were heavily in the tradition of the civil law and the Anglo-American community. During the nineteenth century its edges touched such nations as Japan, Turkey, Persia, Siam, China, and Ethiopia. But generally it had little to do with most of Asia and Africa and with the legal traditions of such major systems as the Islamic, Hindu, Jewish, Chinese, Japanese, African, or Byzantine. It is not surprising, then, that many nations do not think of international law as their law. Indeed some of them are apt to treat it as one more leftover from the days of imperialism.

What can be done about this? The answer is plain: World law must be based on the legal traditions of all parts of the world, not just of one part. As will be seen in the next chapter, the stage is already set for this move, because the statute of the International Court of Justice lists as one of the three major sources of law to be applied by the court, "the general principles of law recognized by civilized nations."

*New concept of content:* World law must rapidly adapt itself to a number of contemporary developments bearing on the problem of peace, such as space law, atomic energy, and international propaganda. To cover these newer subjects, a conscious acceleration of the international law-making process is called for, both through treaties and through the activities of international organizations.

During most of the history of international law the principal source of law has been international custom. This will of course continue to be an important factor. For example, the basis was laid for one of the most important principles of space law—that of the freedom of space—when the first Russian satellite passed over the territories of all the nations of the world without protest. Similarly, the actions of the United Nations force in the Congo have probably contributed to the development of customary international law on the conditions and scope of United Nations military action. But the rapid increase in the number of nations which must be considered, the number of legal systems they represent, and the range and variety of problems to be dealt with necessitate a studied effort to enrich, diversify, and universalize international law through such efforts as the discovery through research of "the general principles of law recognized by civilized nations" and the deliberate blanketing of troublesome areas with carefully thought-out treaties and conventions.

# (4)
# "The General Principles of Law Recognized by Civilized Nations"

PRIMARY SOURCES OF INTERNATIONAL LAW, according to Article 38, paragraph 1, of the Statute of the International Court of Justice, are: (a) international conventions; (b) international custom, as evidence of a general practice accepted as law; and (c) the general principles of law recognized by civilized nations. A fourth category, designated as subsidiary, embraces judicial decisions and the teachings of the most highly qualified publicists.

Of the three major sources of international law, the "general principles" was the last to be officially recognized and is the least developed. The phrase indicates that, if there can be found a common thread running through the internal legal principles of the world's great legal systems, these essentially internal principles become raised to the status of international law. In other words, if we can look inside the legal systems of the world's civilized nations and find certain common principles, we can then add together the sum total of these "inside" principles and get something that is international law.

It can be seen that this source of law has two striking advantages. First, it goes a long way toward solving the problem of making all nations feel that world law is their law. Second, it vastly enlarges the scope and variety of law that can be brought to bear on typical current international controversies.

There has been some misunderstanding among international lawyers on the meaning and scope of the "general principles" clause. Some authorities have expressed the opinion that this clause adds very little to existing law and practice of international communities. Others see the possibility of greatly enriching the content of international law by systematically exploring the common elements in the domestic jurisprudence of the different countries of the world. In spite of this difference of opinion, however, there seems to be a strong majority opinion that these "general principles" do potentially constitute a substantial addition to international law. Obviously the phrase was not intended to refer only to domestic decisions directly applicable to the relations between states, since in this sense it would have been redundant and would have added nothing to international law. On the other hand, the clause clearly does not refer to vague moral principles, since it is couched in terms of actual principles of law. The main body of scholarly and judicial opinion on this clause, then, holds that the clause refers to those principles developed in domestic law which can be carried over and applied by analogy to international questions. The agreement must be general, although it perhaps does not have to be unanimous. Moreover, the clause does not refer to concrete, particularized rules of law, but to general principles, and for this reason a specific, technical rule of law, even if it happened to be universal, would not necessarily be rigidly controlling on the International Court.

Thus, one of the most elementary general principles would be the keeping of agreements. Here is a principle that lies at the foundation of every legal system worthy of the name. Moreover, it has direct application to international law, since agreements in the form of treaties make up a large part of the conduct of international relations. But a principle can be less broad and still be treated as "general." For example, if it were found that the major legal systems agree that, when the first party to a contract makes it impossible for the second party to perform, the second party is excused from his obligation, this could undoubtedly be applied to international treaties.

The distinction between principles and rules is useful in dispelling a common misconception that the world's legal systems are all so diverse that it would be hopeless to look for any kind of significant consensus. This misconception repeatedly crops up in debates about acceptance of the International Court's jurisdiction by the United States or other countries. Uninformed critics of the Court are constantly asking, "How can we entrust our rights to a Court made up of judges from all kinds of different legal backgrounds, and how can we suppose that they understand our ideas of justice?"

Perhaps the reason for this misapprehension is the fact that, when we read of other cultures and systems, it is usually the picturesque differences that receive the most attention. On close examination it will be found that these differences, so far as law is concerned, lie principally in three areas: ritualistic practices, the distribution and descent of property, and marital and other domestic relations. We read fascinating books by Margaret Mead and Ruth Benedict, and we raise our eyebrows over the quaint customs of these distant people, such as forbidding women to eat bananas on pain of strangulation; and then we jump to the conclusion that we cannot possibly have anything in common with such people, so far as law is concerned.

However, when we come to the great principles that are relevant to the problem of peace and that have potential application by analogy to international conduct, we begin to discover that there is a reassuring degree of agreement. On reflection we begin to realize that this is not so surprising after all. Sooner or later, as human beings go about their daily affairs—buying and selling, preserving order and security, protecting their families and their rights—common sense and conscience will relentlessly hammer out principles of conduct whose general shape is familiar in any part of the world.

In the next few chapters, following the approach suggested by Jenks in *The Common Law of Mankind,* an attempt will be made to show the potentialities and promise of the general principles approach in relation to seven major concepts having specific application to the problem of peace and war: sovereignty within the law; the limits on the right of self-defense, as applied to the problem of aggression; the circumstances under which one party can terminate an agreement; liability for illegal harm, including use of words to harm, as in propaganda; protection of acquired rights, with its application to international investment; the duty to consult before affecting the rights

of others, with possible applications to such problems as
rights in international rivers; and the principle of third-
party determination of disputes, with implications for the
subject of judicial independence and of recognition of international judicial processes.

# (5)
## Sovereignty Under the Law

ONE OF THE ROADBLOCKS TO WORLD PEACE
in this nationalistic era is the notion that a national sovereign is not within the law but is the ultimate source of
law. If this idea were true, it would follow there could
not be any kind of international law or order binding on
any national ruler.

But this belief is not true. The deepest traditions of the
world's major legal systems (with the possible exception
of the Soviet) hold that the sovereign of any particular
state is not above the law. This may seem surprising at
first, since we have become so used to assertions of the
right of sovereignty in international law and of the rights
of nationalism in international politics. But the cause for
surprise disappears when we remember that most great
legal systems such as the Jewish law or Hindu law or
Islamic law have their roots in a religious tradition, or
something resembling it such as a natural law concept.
After all, would any potentate who happened to occupy
a throne in the Islamic world dare to stand up and say,
"I am above the Law of Islam"?

The most familiar illustration is an Old Testament story which we all know, but whose legal significance we may never have appreciated: the story of King Ahab and Naboth's vineyard.

All King Ahab wanted was to acquire a nearby vineyard belonging to Naboth. Ahab was king in Israel. Naboth was a plain citizen. Ahab was quite reasonable—he was even willing to pay for the vineyard. But Naboth invoked the Jewish Law of Inheritance, which was above both king and commoner. "The Lord forbid it me, that I should give the inheritance of my fathers unto thee," said Naboth. What did Ahab say? Did he say, "I'm the sovereign around here. I make the laws."? He did not. "He laid him down upon his bed, and turned away his face, and would eat no bread."—I Kings 21.

At this point entered Jezebel. In one scornful phrase Jezebel summed up the attitude of all those before and since who have thought that the sovereign was above the law:

"Dost thou now govern the kingdom of Israel?"

Jezebel was what might be called an early type of legal positivist. And we all know what happened to Jezebel. The searing wrath of Jehovah, the appalling punishments visited upon one who would defy the law of Israel leave no doubt where this particular legal tradition stands on the question of sovereignty under the law.

In Hindu law is encountered the same principle. K. A. N. Sastri, writing in *The Indian Yearbook of International Affairs* (1953), Volume 2, page 140, says:

Mention may be made also of the Indian conception of law and sovereignty which applies to the field of international law as much as to state law. For the Indian theorist of old, law derived its validity from its conformity to Dharma; Dharma is linked up both historically and logically with a Vedic concept of Rita or universal order of the nature of things. The nearest approach to this in Western thought is found in the idea of the law of nature in its conformity to right reason. . . . The King . . . is as much subject to law as all the others in the state, and law is the true sovereign. And this view of the supremacy or sovereignty of law applies to all political relations, including those among different states.

In Islamic law the same principle is found. According to N. C. Sen-Gupta, in *Evolution of Ancient Indian Law* (1953):

The ancient Aryan did not look upon the king as either the source or even the repository of law. . . . The duty of the king to maintain and uphold that law was itself imposed upon him by that law.

H. A. R. Gibbs, writing in *Law in the Middle East* (1955), by Majid Khadduri and Herbert Liebesny, asserts:

There can be no "sovereign state" in the sense that the state has the right of enacting its own law, though it may have some freedom in determining its constitutional structure. The law precedes the state, both logically and in terms of time, and a state exists for the whole purpose of maintaining and enforcing the law.

In African tribal law the tradition is similar. T. O. Elias, in *The Nature of African Customary Law* (1956), says:

It may at first seem that societies with an hierarchical system of chieftaincy and particularly those in which there are kings at their heads, the rulers must necessarily be despots. The institution of kingship or chiefship is, except among certain tribes, generally regarded as sacred in African society; but no holder of either office is in the political thinking of the people above the law on that account.

Along the same line R. S. Rattray, in *Ashanti Law and Constitution* (1929), states:

> The position of the modern ruler has altered but little. . . . His person, just so long as he is on the Stool, is sacred. In spite of this reverence and religious awe, however, his subjects always had very distinct ideas as to the manner in which he could exercise his authority constitutionally.

As to ancient Chinese law, Siu Tchoan-Pao, in *Le Droit des Gens et la Chine Antique* (1924), is authority for the statement that Lao-Tze, Confucius, and Mencius all denied the absoluteness of sovereignty and insisted on legal restrictions on its exercise.

It is hardly necessary to cite authority for the proposition that the English common law placed the law above the sovereign. The famous encounter between Sir Edward Coke and James I is one of the great episodes of English history. The king, in a rage, charged that Coke was in effect contending that the king was under the law, "which it were treason to affirm." In the teeth of this far-from-subtle threat the chief justice, citing Henry de Bracton, replied that "the King ought not to be under any man, but under God and the law."

As for the civil law, the story can best perhaps be summed up by a quotation from Léon Duguit in Chapter I of *Law in the Modern State* (1919):

Sovereignty goes back in its origin to Roman Law. During the feudal period it was almost completely eclipsed. . . . There are innumerable social and political facts with which the revolutionary theory of sovereignty is incompatible. . . . Any system of public law can be vital only so far as it is based on a given sanction to the following rules: first, the holders of power cannot do certain things; second, there are certain things they must do.

This final sentence appears to reflect the dominant civil law attitude today.

The one system that perhaps does not fit in with this pattern is the Soviet legal system. T. A. Taracousio says that sovereignty must be viewed "as a paramount proletarian right for international social reconstruction manifested temporarily in national self-determination and class struggle."

At this point one can only observe that Soviet jurisprudence is constantly shifting and changing and express the hope that, for reasons discussed in Chapter 21, the process of change will lessen the distance between Soviet and other systems of legal thought.

This summary drawn from various legal systems should not be taken to deny the existence of formidable difficulties, but it is intended merely to establish a prima facie showing of the possibility of a fruitful carry-over of general principles of domestic law on sovereignty to the international scene. The difficulties are those associated with the upsurge of nationalistic thought and sentiment in many parts of the world. To some extent the philosophical concept of "positive law" is also associated with the idea of sovereignty above the law.

At the risk of seeming to sum up an immensely complex and controversial field of jurisprudence in an oversimplified dictum, one might venture this general statement: The idea that the sovereign is under the law is both the oldest and the youngest legal tradition. By contrast, the idea of sovereignty above the law and of Austinian positive law occupies a position that has neither the respectability of antiquity nor the cogency of modernity. It is a safe statement that, among legal philosophers today, there are few who accept the legal positivism of Hegel, Hobbes, and Austin. On the practical side, any new country which is about to take its stand on this issue of sovereignty is confronted with this choice: If it consults its own deepest legal traditions, it will find an emphatic assertion of the principle that the sovereign is under the law. If, on the other hand, the country aspires to emulate the most advanced and highly developed countries of the world, it will discover that these more advanced countries have long since put the concept of absolute sovereignty behind them and are in the vanguard of progress toward law and organization that rises above national boundaries. And so, while the first impulse of a new nation might be to assert its sovereignty to the hilt, a more mature consideration could reveal that the principle of sovereignty under the law has both the deepest roots and the most up-to-date validity.

Among the evidences of the modern ascendancy of this principle are the writings of leading scholars such as Hans Kelsen, Roscoe Pound, and Léon Duguit. Another evidence is the line of decisions of the International Court. Sir Hersch Lauterpacht, in *The Development of Inter-*

*national Law,* discusses in considerable detail the decisions
of the Permanent Court of International Justice that set
the tone of limitation of sovereignty which necessarily had
to emerge if the Court was to be effective. Still other
highly significant evidence of the modern attitude lies in
the provisions of the new constitutions of such countries
as France, the Netherlands, and the Federal Republic of
Germany, all of which place world law above domestic
law by explicit language stating that the obligations of
treaties cannot be undone by the act of the national legislature. In Japan the new 1946 constitution states:

No nation is responsible to itself alone but the laws of political morality are universal and obedience to such laws is
incumbent upon all nations which would sustain their sovereignty and justify their sovereign relationship with other
nations.

Of course, a demonstration that sovereignty under the
law is a general principle recognized by civilized nations,
no matter how successful, will not in itself create a system of world legal order. What it would do is to "break
the ice" and get past the first barrier, which is the conception of the absoluteness of nationalistic sovereignty. The
carry-over of this principle onto the international scene
cannot be completely accomplished by any single formula,
but would take the form of identifying the imperatives of
international conduct with "the law" which each system
recognizes to be above any particular sovereign. An example of how this parallel can be drawn may be seen in
the article by Sastri previously cited. He says at page 141:

Among modern Western writers on law, Krabbe may be
said to furnish a close parallel to this ancient line of Indian

thought. For according to him, acts of state are legitimate and valid only to the extent that they conform to the rule of law. International law comes into existence when people from different states, under the impact of external events, widen their sense of right choice to include international relations. The resulting rules of international law constitute real law. Their source is not the will of the states but the consciousness of law felt by those individuals whose interests are affected by the rule, or who as members are called upon to take care of those interests. National and international law, therefore, have essentially the same quality, and both are superior to state rule as such.

# (6)
# Aggression and the Limits of Self-Defense

A SECOND GENERAL PRINCIPLE WHICH MAY be of help on the international scene is that governing aggression and self-defense.

For years the problem of defining aggression has been baffling the world. Men have been struggling with this question ever since St. Augustine drew a distinction between just and unjust war in order to reconcile with Christian principle the necessity of meeting with force the pagan barbarian invasions of the fourth century. The outlawing of war, first in the Kellogg-Briand Pact and most recently in the United Nations Charter, is weakened in its practical application by the absence of an agreed and workable definition of the distinction between aggression and self-defense.

Perhaps one reason for our present difficulty is that "aggression" is a fighting word. If it is said to a nation, "Let us discuss what aggression is in order to see whether you are guilty of it," the nation is immediately insulted and walks out.

The "general principles" approach may have a part to play in getting around this difficulty. The key may be to center the discussion, not on "aggression," but on "the limitations of the right of self-defense." After all, any aggressor nowadays will say that he was acting in self-defense and that, therefore, he is within an exception to the outlawing of force specifically recognized by the United Nations Charter.

Suppose, then, we accept for the sake of argument the claim of self-defense. That is not the end of the story. We can then say to the alleged aggressor: "You say you were acting in self-defense. But there are definite limitations on self-defense recognized by all civilized nations including your own. You must observe those limitations if you want to rely on the plea of self-defense."

These limitations are three:

1. There must be a reasonable apprehension of danger.
2. The force used to meet the danger must be proportionate to the real or apprehended danger.
3. The reasonableness of the apprehension and of the amount of force used to meet it must be subject to impartial determination by a third-party tribunal.

It is a striking fact of world law that practically every legal system, including the Soviet, agrees on these principles. There is some variation in the extent to which self-defense is encouraged and in the amount of force that would be accepted as reasonable in practice. But the principles themselves may be found stated in the common law, in civil law codes such as the German, Italian, and French, in Islamic law, in the Jewish Code of Maimonides, in the Indian Penal Code, in Chinese law, in Japanese law, in African law, and in the Soviet Penal Code, Article 19.

The reason these principles are common is that they are based on common sense. Suppose my neighbor and I have an argument. Suppose he is a poor, run-down weakling weighing 120 pounds, while I am a professional wrestler. In his excitement he slaps my face with the tips of his flabby fingers. Obviously this creates in me a right of self-defense. But how far can I go? Can I break his arm? Can I go on and choke him to death? Can I enter his house, tie him down, and take over his house and possessions? Of course not. The most I can do is to apply as much restraint as is needed to keep him from hurting me, and that, in these circumstances, would not be much.

That this illustration may have some contemporary relevance is evident from a remark dropped by Premier Nikita Khrushchev in 1960. He said that in Soviet doctrine, unlike Christian doctrine, the response to a slap was not to turn the other cheek but to knock the other fellow's head off.

The significance for the problem of aggression is clear. The big, powerful nation which overruns its tiny neighbor by force or threats of force will probably say that this is necessary in self-defense. But if, under the big nation's own law, the force must be proportionate to the threat, how can anyone contend that the appropriate force must include killing hundreds of people, terrorizing the small country with tanks, and then subjecting the victim to permanent occupation and loss of personal and national freedom?

The third factor, that of independent third-party judgment on the necessity for and reasonableness of the use of force in self-defense, rests on the universal acceptance of the idea that disputes must be decided by an impartial third person. It is clear enough that the limitations on self-defense would not mean much if the offending country could make a final decision which could not be questioned by anyone else. Yet this is exactly what German defendants tried to contend in the Nuremberg trials. They claimed that Germany's aggressions were preventive action necessitated by threats from other nations and that it had a right to decide that fact conclusively for itself. The International Military Tribunal rejected this claim on the ground that with this theory there could never be any enforcement of international law. The same decision was made by the International Military Tribunal for the Far East at Tokyo. In these two decisions can be seen a clear case of the translation onto the international scene of a general principle of law recognized by civilized nations, in the crucial area of deciding the existence of aggression.

# (7)
# Obligation and Termination of Treaties

THE THIRD GENERAL PRINCIPLE OF KEY IM-
portance to world peace is the principle that agreements
must be kept. It is through treaties that nations nowadays
adjust their most important affairs. Boundary agreements,
treaties of peace, treaties of commerce strongly affecting
economic interests—these and dozens of other kinds of
treaties go to the very heart of the way nations get along
with respect to their highest national interests. For the
same reason, behind almost every serious case of international tension will be found claims of breach of treaty
or other international obligation. A recent example is the
Berlin crisis, which centers around the charge that the
USSR's announced intention to turn over its role under
the Four-Power Agreement to East Germany is a breach
of its obligations under that treaty.

Thus, any help that can be drawn from the "general
principles of law recognized by civilized nations" in less-
ening the strife that grows out of claimed breaches of
treaties would be of first-line significance in the cause of
peace.

The broad principle—agreements must be kept—is
universally accepted. Indeed it would be difficult to imagine a legal system of a civilized country that did not begin with this as its bedrock foundation. The words of

the Koran, "Oh ye who believe, fulfill your pledges," are echoed throughout the world's legal systems, right down to the words of Andrei Vyshinski, who said of treaties: "The Soviet theory of international law considers treaties . . . to be the main source of international law. Their legal significance and validity must be unconditionally observed."

With this unanimity on the sanctity of agreements, why then is there so much recrimination about going back on promises? Why has our State Department been able to compile a whole book full of alleged violations of treaties by Communist nations? It is not that the sanctity of treaties has been expressly flouted. Once in a great while some ruthless politician may call a treaty a scrap of paper, but this is a rarity. What often happens is that one of the parties, while affirming the general binding force of agreements, will then go on to assert that under some legal doctrine of termination the particular obligation no longer exists.

If a country feels free to improvise legal theories which supposedly discharge it from its treaty obligations, the binding force of treaties can become an illusion. On the other hand, if the general principles accepted by major legal systems in the law of contracts contain an objective standard by which to judge when an agreement may be deemed ended, it would be reasonable to confront any country with this principle and insist that it be respected.

One illustration—perhaps the most important—will show how this would work out. This has to do with the question of when an agreement may be deemed released by a change in circumstances. Every mature legal system has evolved a principle to the general effect that a contract may be dissolved by a change in conditions which makes it impossible for one party to perform, through no fault of his own. In English law this doctrine is associated with the famous "Coronation Cases." In England, whenever there is a coronation procession, the people who are lucky enough to own houses along the route make a tidy profit by renting out seats on their balconies or in their windows. When Edward VII became king in 1901, his official coronation was set for a date in 1902. Because of his illness the coronation had to be put off, and the procession did not take place as planned. Naturally, hundreds of contracts that had been made on the assumption of a coronation were "frustrated," and the people who had rented seats for the procession or made other contracts based on the coronation refused to pay. The upshot was a series of decisions laying down the general proposition that when both parties to a contract make their agreement on the mutual assumption of a given fact, and through neither party's fault that fact turns out to be nonexistent, the obligation is discharged.

Similar doctrines have resulted from impossibility of performance because of, for example, intervening outbreak of war. This general type of principle is familiar in civil law countries and also in countries like India and some Islamic nations where common or civil law has had an influence on contract law. The Soviet Civil Code contains two definite provisions on the question of when an agreement is discharged by change in conditions. The first provision is that nonperformance is excused if performance was made impossible by circumstances that the party could not prevent. The second provision states that a party is excused if the impossibility came about because of the negligence or deliberate act of the other party.

By contrast with these fairly definite principles, on the international scene one encounters a sort of magic formula that is sometimes invoked when one country decides it would like to get out of its obligation. The magic words are *rebus sic stantibus.* This means roughly "as long as things remain the same." The implication is that any treaty is binding only so long as the conditions or assumptions under which it was made remain unchanged.

Thus, the Soviet Union, wanting to get out of the Four-Power Agreement on Berlin, might argue that the original agreement was a postwar occupation arrangement, that the war has been over for more than fifteen years, and that therefore the passage of time and change in conditions have altered the obligations of the treaty. One reason Russia has not pushed this argument too hard may be that the Potsdam Agreement was made about the same time—and Russia very much wants to keep that treaty alive. Another reason may be that the *rebus sic stantibus* principle itself does not seem to be accepted in current Soviet legal theory.

Everyone would agree that some kind of principle is necessary to temper the rigid application of a contract or treaty in cases of frustration or impossibility. On the other hand, if agreements are not to become a farce, the principles governing release must themselves be reasonably clear and objective. Merely to say "conditions have changed" is hardly a definite enough test. Conditions are always changing. Significantly, the principle of *rebus sic stantibus* has never been recognized by the International Court of Justice.

To find a test that is definite enough, we would do well to start with the contract rules just mentioned. Instead of talking vaguely of change of conditions, we might then be able to "nail down" three or four or five specific kinds of change in condition that are recognized as grounds for discharge.

Here again, as in the case of self-defense, there must also be the added element of third-party judgment. There will be many complex and close questions surrounding these principles, but the first step would be to find a sufficiently agreed set of principles to give the third-party tribunal something from which to deduce its particular decisions.

# (8)
# Illegal Harm

THE NEXT GENERAL PRINCIPLE IS: TO DO unjustified harm to one's neighbor is a legal wrong.

When the matter is stated like this, it sounds self-evident. And yet—strange as it seems—the story of law shows that it is only in the highly developed legal systems that there finally emerges an all-inclusive principle forbidding harm, as distinguished from a specific list of prohibited acts.

If one goes back to the earliest code, that of Hammurabi in Babylon of 2100 B.C., he will find a detailed list of wrongs and corresponding payments. It is amusing to find such curiosities as the exact payment when a cock belonging to the defendant crows so loudly as to break a vessel belonging to the plaintiff.

In the dawn of every other legal system, including the English, the same appears to have been true. The oldest English law book is that containing the laws of Ethelbert, King of Kent, from about 600 A.D. Here again one encounters the detailed catalog of prices placed on selected morsels of mischief: pulling someone's hair, fifty scaetts; fingernails or toenails, one shilling per nail; and so on for twenty-eight sections of particular kinds of injuries.

Modern law has only recently begun to emerge from this period, even in the common-law countries. An argument can still be raised among legal scholars on whether there is a general Law of Tort, or only a Law of Torts. It is not surprising, then, that the world's legal systems are now to be found at various way-stations along this road to a general principle of unlawful harm. Islamic law, for example, seems to be still in the specific-harm stage but definitely moving in the direction of a general theory of liability. The civil law codes of Europe and the Soviet Civil Code plainly accept the general principle of wrongful harm.

What is the significance to world law? With all the new ways of causing harm that are now at our disposal, we need a broad principle of liability for harm and cannot get along with a primitive list of items which have been singled out for prohibition in earlier law.

Take radio propaganda, for example. The nature of

this modern problem can be illustrated by an incident involving the late Prime Minister of Iraq, Nuri as-Said. The writer paid a call on him early in 1957 in the course of United States Information Agency duties. The door was hardly closed when Nuri barked out, "I want some jamming equipment."

"But, Mr. Prime Minister, you know that the United States doesn't believe in jamming. Our belief in freedom of speech . . ."

"Oh, that's all right for you, but I want some jamming equipment, and I need it fast. Let me tell you why. Not long ago there was a broadcast from Radio Cairo beamed at Baghdad. The broadcast said that I, Nuri, with my own hands, had just murdered four of the holiest men of Islam right in the Holy Mosque over across the river. What do you suppose happened? Rioting, bloodshed, killing, all over the place. I can't have that sort of thing. I want some jamming equipment."

We hear of such incidents from time to time, some going even so far as to call on a people by international radio to kill their own king. Now, if this is to be a world of law, are these activities legal or illegal?

If you stand on the boundary and throw a rock into another country with intent to injure or kill, this would obviously be an offense. If you lobbed explosive shells into the other country with intent to cause injury and death, this too is plainly a wrong in international law. Suppose, then, you send electronic radio impulses into the other country with intent to cause rioting, bloodshed, injury, and death. Should this be any less an offense merely because the mechanism is more modern and more subtle?

The offender might argue that there is no explicit provision of international law violated—just as some ancient malefactor might contend that, while pulling hair and breaking arms were prohibited, there was no law against his pouring a can of paint over the plaintiff. But in a modern system of world law any such primitive contention seems out of place. Conventional international law needs to be supplemented by drawing upon the general principles recognized by civilized nations.

When we do this, we begin to discover that there are some general principles that give a clue to the radio propaganda problem. The use of words to cause harm is a familiar kind of wrong. The principle that the person who incites the commission of an injury is himself liable is equally familiar. So by piecing together these elementary principles—not by searching for a specific law forbidding use of radio as such to cause injury—one can begin to demonstrate that world law is capable of adapting itself to the newer kinds of wrongdoing.

We saw the same kind of progression in the common law doctrine of nuisance. This doctrine recognized quite early that it was just as much a nuisance to send dense smoke onto your neighbor's property as to throw chunks of rock from a dynamiting operation. But even subtler vehicles of harm were gradually recognized. Foul smells, for example. Dust and noise. Even vibrations and shocks. And so the earth tremor from dynamiting might be just as real a nuisance as the rock flying through the air.

On the scale of international wrongdoing the potential questions arising from new sources of damage are obvious: fall-out from atomic explosions, pollution by disposition of atomic waste, falling fragments of missiles or space vehicles, and so on. The solution, if there is to be one, must be sought in general principles of law recognized by civilized nations, at least until the field can be adequately covered by agreed codes of conduct tailored to the exact problem—an approach discussed in a later chapter.

# (9)
# Other General Principles Relevant to Peace

FOUR EXAMPLES HAVE BEEN GIVEN OF general principles with special bearing upon world peace: sovereignty under the law, limits on self-defense, termination of treaties, and illegal harm. Three more such general principles may now be briefly noted, with an indication of the point at which they may have a specific impact in their international version. Since these specific applications are discussed from other points of view elsewhere in this book, they will be merely noted here to show the link with the "general principles" approach.

## Third-Party Adjudication

One of the most fundamental and widespread of all legal principles is the principle of third-party determination of disputes. Declarations of this principle, together with specific commands to carry it into force, can be found in the Code of Maimonides, in ancient Hindu law, in the Koran, in the Soviet Code of Civil Procedure, in the Chinese Code of Civil Procedure, in African law, and in every other legal system. Among the applications of the principle that may be found in these sources are penalties for judges who hold private conversations with one of the parties or who decide cases on the testimony of only one party. Indeed, the Code of Maimonides forbids even the most subtle kinds of discrimination in the course of a hearing, such as "not permitting one to state his case at length and telling the other to be brief, not to show courtesy to one, speaking softly to him, and frown upon the other, addressing him harshly. . . . One of the litigants must not be allowed to be seated and the other kept standing; but both should be standing. . . ."

In practice, however, the extent to which this principle is successful depends to a considerable degree on the extent of judicial independence within the particular country's governmental system. Here we find that the highly developed conception of the independence of the judiciary (which we take for granted in Anglo-American jurisprudence), although it is reflected in the Asian countries sharing the British tradition, is departed from in varying degrees in most other systems. When we get to the Soviet system, we find a writer like Nikolai Krylenko telling us that "the Court is an organ of state administration and as such does not differ in its nature from any other organs of state administration which are designed, as the Court is, to carry out one and the same governmental policy."

On the international level the principle of judicial independence has been realized to a substantial degree in the International Court of Justice. The judges are elected by an elaborate and careful procedure designed to bring out the best judicial talent available, and they hold their offices nine years. As will be seen later, the actual record of their decisions demonstrates a high degree of integrity and independence. It is possible that this independence could be strengthened even further by such devices as making terms of office even longer. But, on the whole, the present problem is not so much to build independence into the judicial institution itself as to get all the countries of the world to accept the judicial institution having this independence. This problem of acceptance is the subject of Part Three of this book. The main point to be noted here is that, as pointed out by Jenks in *The Common Law of Mankind:*

It may perhaps be significant that countries where the judiciary is least independent are among the most reluctant to accept the compulsory jurisdiction of the International Court, partly because they neither believe in nor understand the nature of its independence and partly because they are not accustomed, except in matters of a private law character, to submitting to the test of independent judicial decision.

## Acquired Rights

Another widespread general legal principle, of marked importance to the strengthening of peace by economic development of newer countries, is the principle of respect for and protection of acquired rights. Even in a modern

Communist society, the inexorable necessity of ordering relations between individuals inevitably produces this kind of protection of rights. It is interesting to watch this process working itself out in the Soviet Union. Any idea that communism rejects the idea of "property," whatever validity it may have for communism of the Utopian type, does not fit the facts of the Soviet Union that we see today. Members of the increasingly large middle class in the Soviet Union are becoming accustomed to having a *dacha* in the country, an apartment in town, household goods and appliances of considerable value, and perhaps an automobile. The everyday rights to own, use, sell, buy, bequeath, and in some cases even rent such property are protected by law in much the same way as they would be anywhere else. There are some differences, mostly stemming from the Communist aversion to acquiring private income from property. However, even these differences are so erratic that they leave no clear impression of principle. For example, it is perfectly possible to rent a house or even to divide a house into apartments and rent them. On the other hand, for some reason, it is not permitted to rent a piece of personal property such as an automobile. Other differences from the general principles accepted by most nations would include the destruction of pre-Revolutionary vested rights and a broad principle that rights are not protected if exercised in contradiction to their social and economic purpose. This last concept, depending on interpretation, may have a greater or less resemblance to the principle of "abuse of rights," which is more widely accepted in some other legal systems than it is in the English and American.

When we come to the application of the principle of protection of acquired rights to international affairs, we find that the key question is one in which there is no clear guide at the present stage of development of law among the various systems. This question is the extent of the right of governments to take private property in the public interest, and particularly the accompanying duties of the government to provide adequate safeguards and compensation. This subject is discussed in a later chapter. It is because the general principles of law in their present state of evolution are not adequate to supply a firm basis of law for the protection of international investment that this problem can more effectively be approached through the traditional sources of international law—custom and treaties.

## Duty of Consultation

The final general principle that may be mentioned is the duty of consultation before taking action affecting the interests of others. An interesting feature of this principle is the fact that it appears to be more highly developed in Asian and African legal systems than in the Anglo-American system and, accordingly, can serve as a useful corrective to any notion that the sharing of general principles of law is a one-sided affair. Although Anglo-American law has undergone a considerable process of softening and tempering on this point, it seemed to take as its starting point the proposition that legal rights were legal rights and that as long as one stayed within his legal rights he did not have to consult anyone or apologize to anyone. Thus, if I wanted to pump all the water out of an underground stream passing under my property, and if I thus ruined my neighbor's water supply, my motives for doing so were nobody's business, provided I remained on my own property and merely exercised my legal right to pump the water that flowed under my property. Similarly, if I had a legal grievance against my neighbor, I had a perfect legal right to drag him into court without any preliminaries and demand legal satisfaction. However, in various other legal systems including Chinese, Japanese, African, Hindu, Jewish, and Soviet, there can be found in some degree the principle that there is obligation to talk matters over with the people to be affected before some action is taken affecting their interests. In Chinese and Japanese law, in particular, there appears to be an actual obligation to attempt conciliation before carrying a dispute to the length of actual legal suit.

It is interesting that this principle of consultation has now begun to play a part in several important international areas. Most of the members of the United Nations are members of the International Monetary Fund and parties to the General Agreement on Tariffs and Trade and, as such, are legally bound to engage in mutual consultation before taking action affecting another member's interests in either the field of currency or the field of tariffs.

The problem of disputes over international waters, already mentioned in connection with a need to make international law materials more accessible, could also profit by an approach based on this general principle of consultation. At the present time, and for the remainder of this century, water seems likely to be one of the world's most important resources. Just as within most regions of the United States, even those areas previously thought of as "well watered," so in country after country the problem of adequate water resources has become increasingly vital with population growth and the tremendously growing demand for water brought about by a rapidly industrializing civilization. International complications arise because so many streams and lakes lie along, or flow across, international boundaries. The number of situations causing such international complications has been increased by the political upheavals of recent years which have resulted in some formerly wholly national river basins becoming bisected by new political boundaries. To the earlier international controversies concerning the right to navigate international bodies of water there have been added the competing needs for irrigation, electric power, and use in industry of many kinds. At the present time international discussions are underway seeking settlements to make possible increased utilization of the basins of the Columbia, Colorado, Indus, Nile, Helmand, Uruguay, Tigris-Euphrates, Saint Lawrence (including the Lake Michigan diversion question), Jordan, La Plata, Mekong, Ganges, and Brahmaputra, to mention only the most prominent cases. In the years ahead, these and other cases must be settled or they will reach a critical and explosive stage. It is no exaggeration to say that to large numbers of people some of these disputes are literally a matter of life and death and could easily lead to armed conflict.

The optimum development of these great international

river basins emphatically calls for a wholehearted application of the principle of consultation, since if the countries act entirely independently they may not only lose the
benefit of joint river development but may also affirmatively damage each other's interests. To take an extreme
case, if the upper riparian in some of these instances were
to dam up or divert substantial quantities of water without notice, the result might actually be widespread famine
and death among the people of the lower riparian state
who have come to rely on this water to irrigate their crops.
Or, to take another extreme case, if the upper riparian
state obtained knowledge that severe flood waters were
rushing toward the lower riparian state and did nothing
to warn that state, the result again might be death and destruction which could easily have been avoided. The
Committee on the Uses of Waters of International Rivers
of the American branch of the International Law Association has drawn up a set of suggested principles which are
the focal point of discussion of this association and which
may be taken as a reasonably widely held agreement on
the present state of the "general principles of law" on this
point. Some of the highlights of the statement are as follows:

The riparian has the sovereign right to make the fullest
use of the part of a system of international waters under its
jurisdiction consistent with the corresponding right of each
co-riparian.

The riparian is under duty to refrain from causing a change
in the existing regime of a system of international waters
which would interfere with the exercise by a co-riparian of its
right to share on a just and reasonable basis in the benefits
of the system without first giving the co-riparian an oppor-

tunity to object; and if objection is made, to refrain from causing the change so long as the co-riparian demonstrates its willingness to reach a prompt and just solution by the pacific means envisaged in the Charter of the United Nations, including the determination by the International Court of Justice or other agreed tribunal. . . .

A riparian may not unreasonably withhold from a co-riparian, or refuse to give it access to, data relevant to the termination or observance of their respective rights and duties under the existing regime of the system of international waters, or data with respect to any proposed change in that regime.

Thus it can be seen that one of the main themes of this attempt to regularize the development of international river basins is the general principle of consultation. This is necessarily so, because the optimum economic development of these river basins is not going to come about as a result of rigid and technical insistence on supposed legal rights. Rather, it will require genuine cooperation, not just on legal questions, but on the multitude of other questions, including the engineering, financial, and administrative. There is cause for great hope and promise in the fact that the bitterest rivers dispute of recent times, that between India and Pakistan over the Indus River Basin, was at last settled through the good offices of the International Bank. The settlement is something much more than a mere definition of respect of legal rights; it couples this with a far-ranging, constructive program for maximizing the economic potential of the entire Indus River Basin, to the mutual gain of both India and Pakistan.

These three general principles and their applications to

contemporary international issues, together with the four principles discussed and applied in preceding chapters, will supply seven illustrations of how, by drawing on the deepest wellsprings of principles recognized by civilized nations, we can help to build a new kind of world law which will not only be useful in the disposition of some troublesome issues now causing threats to peace but also have a good chance of finding acceptance among the nations.

# (10)
# Making New Law Through Treaties

No matter how thoroughly we exploit existing international law, including the general principles of law recognized by civilized nations, there will be many gaps that must be filled, particularly with regard to some of the newer and more rapidly developing areas of international relationship. The most effective way to fill them is with agreed codes, conventions, and treaties covering as many nations as possible.

Treaties, which along with customary law and the general principles of law recognized by civilized nations are listed in the International Court Statute as one of the three major sources of international law, share the important modern advantage cited for the "general principles" source. That is, law created by treaty has its own built-in acceptability. It cannot be criticized as the handiwork of other times and other nations. As has been noted in the quotation from Vyshinsky, acceptance of the binding force of treaties is emphatically accepted in Soviet legal theory. The more we can blanket important legal areas with bilateral and multilateral treaties, the more we shall broaden the area of substantive law in which authenticity as law is outside the range of controversy.

A good example of this process in an older area of law is the law of the sea. Two international conferences were held. The first conference reached agreement on practically all questions of the law of the sea except the troublesome question of the width of territorial waters. The traditional three-mile limit has been under attack for some time as being unrealistic in the light of modern conditions. The second conference attempted to reach agreement on this problem of territorial waters and unfortunately failed by only one vote of achieving the necessary majority on a compromise proposal. However, this failure to agree on the width of territorial waters should not obscure the remarkable achievement of securing practically universal acceptance of a modernized code governing a wide range of international law, rules, and principles under the heading of the law of the sea. Similar agreements have for a number of years governed such activities as international operation of aircraft, international postal operations, narcotics and white slave traffic, patents and copyrights, ocean cables, etc.

In 1959 a good start was made on an agreed regime for Antarctica. The treaty entered into marks a notable ad-

vance in reaching agreement among a number of interested states, including the United States, the Soviet Union,
and other countries having claims or interests in the Antarctic. It provides that Antarctica shall be used only for
peaceful purposes, that atomic explosions are forbidden,
and that free access to all installations and aerial inspections by designated personnel shall be permitted. The
treaty is by no means as complete as an ideal treaty might
be. For example, there is no specified procedure other
than consultation for determining whether a breach of the
treaty has occurred. Although the treaty makes it clear
that it does not imply a renunciation of existing territorial
claims, it does provide that there shall be no additional
claims made while the treaty is in force. The working out
of this agreement, in an area which for so long has been
marked by the bitterest kind of disputes, was something
of a minor miracle. The initiative came largely from the
United States, and the success of the negotiations is in
considerable measure a tribute to the statesmanship and
patience of the leaders in the negotiations.

Against this backdrop, the satisfaction occasioned by
the signing of this agreement is tempered somewhat by
the spectacle which followed when the treaty came up
for consent to ratification in the Senate. A determined
attempt was made to destroy the treaty by refusing ratification consent. The treaty was finally ratified with Senate
approval, but the number of opposing votes was substantial enough to serve as a chilling reminder of the magnitude of the job that lies ahead in educating not only the
public but the public's legislative representatives on these
new issues of international law and order. No arguments

of fact or law or substance were adduced by the opponents of ratification. Their attack was almost entirely emotional and rhetorical, sounding the familiar refrains that we are giving up our sovereignty and somehow selling out to the Communists whenever we take another step toward international order under law. Obviously we give up no sovereignty by agreeing that Antarctica should be used only for peaceful purposes and that atomic explosions shall be banned in the area. And when we achieve agreement of free access and aerial inspection, we gain acceptance of a principle and practice which has always been central to our plans for international cooperation, particularly in relation to nuclear testing and disarmament. Explicit provision that existing territorial claims are not detracted from is a sufficient answer to the charge that we are giving up our rights in the Antarctic, and the additional explicit proviso that there shall be no additional claims made while the treaty is in force is a sufficient answer to the charge that the treaty hands over to the Soviet Union something it did not have before.

It would be highly desirable if the same techniques that led to this agreement on Antarctica could be applied in a number of contemporary problem areas, such as the law of atomic energy, the law of international propaganda, the law of international rivers, the protection of private international investment, and the law of outer space. Some of these have been discussed or will be discussed elsewhere in this volume. At this point it might be appropriate to look briefly at the most novel and fascinating of these items—the law of outer space.

Space law is a good example of an area which some

authorities believe can be handled satisfactorily only by anticipating future questions and providing as many answers as possible in advance in a code. The questions that must eventually be answered can only partly be guessed: Is outer space open to anyone who wants to fling an object into it? Are there to be any restrictions on space objects passing "over national territory"? Shall space be limited to peaceful uses? Can it be used for reconnaissance? Who has jurisdiction over space? What laws apply to transactions or wrongs in space? How shall title to the moon, planets, and other objects in space be established, if at all? Will some Columbus drive a flagpole into a parched mountain of the moon and claim the moon for his Isabella? How will traffic be regulated, radio communications kept in order, qualifications for space navigators be established, and standards set for space stations?

Of course, pending the agreement on codes covering these and dozens of other foreseeable questions, one could try to muddle along with analogies from existing law. But the trouble here is that there are at least two possible analogies, neither of which could claim to be clearly binding: the law of the sea and the law of air space. The law of the sea rests on the pervading principle of freedom of the seas. But the law of air space starts from an opposite principle of *usque ad coelum,* or "right up to the sky." The old rule was that, if you owned a piece of land, you also owned an enormous inverted pyramid extending to the center of the earth, and also up to the sky. This served well enough as long as the only questions were rights to dig for minerals or to saw off the limb of your neighbor's tree if it ventured across your property line, how-

ever high in the air it might be. But the advent of air
travel soon changed this concept out of necessity, although the process of change has been painful and is still
causing much uncertainty and litigation. Indeed, the law
of air space is having trouble enough meeting the problems of air transportation without trying to accommodate
space activities.

By a sort of default the Space Age seems to have
started in the general direction of the law of the sea. The
first Sputnik crisscrossed the territory of many nations
without the slightest "by-your-leave," and, more significantly, no one protested. Now all sorts of celestial gar-
bage is whizzing over everyone's national territory, and
the freedom of space seems to be established by acceptance of the accomplished fact. At the moment the pre-
vailing official view both among the major powers and in
the United Nations seems to favor letting events take
their course in the hope, presumably, that other legal questions will answer themselves as the first one did. The
Legal Committee of the United Nations Ad Hoc Committee on Peaceful Uses of Outer Space recently made a
report concluding that a space code is not yet feasible. But
the questions that loom in the distance will not be as easy
or as free from tension as the first one. It is submitted
that, to the extent that we can clearly see certain unavoid-
able legal questions coming, we should get to work on
anticipating and solving them by agreement as soon as
possible. If we wait until someone lands on the moon before starting to discuss what rights are thereby acquired,
it may be too late to expect an amicable solution.

These, then, are some of the jobs and opportunities that await as we strive to supply the first requisite of world law: a well-developed, accessible, and universally acceptable body of law to apply. A striking conclusion that emerges from this analysis is the large part that can be played, in this grim and stormy area of preventing international conflict, by the quiet techniques of scholarship and research at the hands of research centers, universities, professional associations, publishers, business research centers, governmental and international organizations, professors, graduate students, and scholars of all kinds. One thing is plain: there is plenty of work for everyone.

PART TWO

# *The Machinery of World Law*

🮱🮱🮱🮱🮱🮱🮱🮱🮱🮱🮱🮱🮱🮱🮱🮱🮱🮱🮱🮱🮱🮱🮱🮱🮱

## (11)
## Peaceful Legal Settlement— Its Background and History

THE SECOND REQUISITE OF A WORLD LEGAL system is the machinery to administer it.

The principal international court is the International Court of Justice at The Hague. It is the judicial branch of the United Nations, with fifteen distinguished judges, including some of the world's leading international lawyers, on the bench. Its main function is to decide legal disputes between nation-states involving claimed breaches of obligations under international law. It is also empowered to give advisory opinions at the request of the United Nations and certain United Nations agencies. The main problem about the World Court (as it is often called for convenience) is the failure of its member nations to use it. On the average, only about two cases per year have been brought to it, and most of these have had to be turned away by the Court on various grounds relating to jurisdiction. There are a number of reasons for this failure to accord the International Court the role it should play in international affairs. However, in order to present current problems and controversies in meaningful perspective, it is helpful to take a glance backward at the process by which peaceful legal settlement of international disputes has reached the point at which we find it today.

The settlement of international disputes by judicial means is a relatively modern idea. There was something resembling it in ancient Greece, but the use of judicial settlement on a substantial scale begins with the Jay Treaty of 1794 between Great Britain and the United States. This treaty established special commissions to clear up various disputes left after the Revolutionary War, including the question of the proper boundary between Maine and Nova Scotia. Since this episode was such a significant milestone in the story of peaceful legal settlement, it might be interesting to review the story of how this early arbitration came about.

The 1783 Treaty of Peace between the United States and Great Britain fixed the boundaries between the respective territories resulting from the war. One of the lines ran "due north from the source of the Saint Croix River to the high lands" in a wilderness area. Two rivers, known locally as the Maguadavic and the Schoodiac seemed about equally likely to fulfill the description of the Saint Croix on the map the treaty negotiators used. Here was the kind of boundary dispute, coming on the heels of a war, which at some points in history would have been quite capable of plunging the disputants back into war again. The United States and Great Britain chose instead to provide in the Treaty of 1794 for peaceful means of settlement of this and other unresolved issues. Three commissioners were to be appointed with power to make a final decision on the boundary. One commissioner was to be appointed by each party to the treaty and these two were to appoint a third. Their specific task was to decide which river was the Saint Croix and to describe it with particularity, detailing the latitude and longitude of its mouth and source. They were to deliver appropriate documents to the United States and Great Britain, which respectively agreed "to consider such decision as final and conclusive, so as that the same shall never . . . be called into question or made a subject of a dispute or difference between them."

President Washington appointed David Howell, who had been a member of the Supreme Court of Rhode Island. Great Britain appointed Colonel Thomas Barclay, a native of New York and a citizen of Nova Scotia, who had studied law under John Jay and had been speaker of the Provincial Assembly. For the third commissioner they agreed on Judge Egbert Benson of New York, a cousin of Barclay. The commissioners appointed surveyors and actually went to Saint Andrews on Passamaquoddy Bay, into which the two rivers flowed. The British agent naturally argued that the boundary should be the more westerly of the two rivers, and the United States agent stressed the arguments for the more easterly. But as it turned out, the tribunal, composed of men all of whom had been born in places which had become United States territory, reached the unanimous decision that the Saint Croix referred to in the Treaty of Peace was the westerly river. However, they chose the most easterly of its two main branches which came together some distance above its mouth.

Commission and counsel personally explored the area. They "found the western stream large and navigable far up; the eastern small, and interrupted a few miles up by falls." They took the testimony of Indian chiefs. They took the depositions of President John Adams and of John Jay, two of the United States signers of the Treaty of Peace. Historic maps and various other documents were presented in behalf of both parties. Finally, in 1798, the declaration of the commissioners was delivered. There were substantial evidences pointing in both directions, but the decision was carefully placed on such grounds as the intention of the framers of the Treaty of Peace, the historical identity of the river Saint Croix, the effect on existing holdings, forts, and the like, and the achievement of the maximum length of natural boundary line. In concluding this case the agent for the United States made a statement which could well serve as the theme of all who have attempted to follow in the footsteps of this early, successful arbitration: "Why shall not all the nations on earth determine their disputes in this mode, rather than choke the rivers with their carcasses and stain the soil of continents with their slain?"

During the hundred years following the Jay Treaty there was a strong upsurge in the use of arbitration in international disputes. One hundred seventy-seven major disputes between nations were resolved by this means, including seventy-nine to which the United States was a party. It is worth noting that many of these arbitrations involved issues on which public feeling ran high, in which substantial interests were at stake, and in which it was no easy matter for the loser to accept with good grace the decision which he could not be compelled by superior force to obey. One of the most famous arbitrations was the settlement between the United States and England of claims growing out of the depredations of the vessel "Alabama" during the Civil War. In this arbitration Britain was required to pay, and did pay, $15,500,000 damages. On the other hand, in 1871 the United States lost an arbitration to England when the Halifax Commission made an award of $5,500,000 in gold as additional compensation to Great Britain for a fisheries concession under the Convention of 1818. It is worth noting that the United States agent felt so strongly that the award was wrong that he filed a reservation against the validity of the award, but nevertheless the United States government recognized the award and paid it. Again, in 1892, the United States lost another arbitration to Great Britain on the question of its right to police the North Pacific in order to preserve seals from extermination. The United States argued that the Bering Sea, because of rights and customs inherited from Russian sovereignty, was a closed sea under United States jurisdiction. It also argued that the seals were not wild animals but domestic animals wandering out of bounds and hence subject to regulation even beyond territorial waters. The tribunal gave a clear decision against the United States. However, the arbitrators provided regulations for the protection of the seals.

Up to this point in the story the handling of peaceful legal settlement of international disputes, although remarkably effective in the form to which it had evolved at that point, fell short of modern conceptions of international dispute-settling in two respects: the usual device was arbitration rather than adjudication, and the tribunals were ordinarily constituted for one dispute at a time.

Arbitration and adjudication are essentially both methods of judicial settlement. However, they usually have these differences: an arbitration tribunal is normally temporary, set up by the parties for a particular dispute or set of disputes, while a court is permanent; the membership of an arbitration tribunal is chosen by the parties, while that of a court is constituted without reference to the parties' wishes; an arbitral tribunal can be instructed to decide on the basis specified by the parties, but a court decides on the basis of international law; an arbitral proceeding is preceded by an agreement between the parties on the exact issues and the scope of the tribunal's authority, while a court would ordinarily decide for itself what issues are relevant. Nevertheless, the principle is the same: A dispute is laid before an impartial third-party tribunal to be decided according to impartial rules and principles.

The next step forward was an attempt to put arbitration on a more permanent, organized footing, so as to overcome in some degree the second deficiency noted above, that of having to start from the very beginning every time an arbitration was to take place. The first

Hague Conference in 1899 resulted in an agreement by the powers represented there to use their best efforts to insure peaceful settlement of their differences. They created the Permanent Court of Arbitration, which was not a fixed body of men to pass on all cases, but a panel of one hundred fifty to two hundred persons from which arbitrators could be chosen for any particular controversy. This court is still technically in existence but has not been used much in recent years. While it handled only about twenty cases, some of them were of substantial gravity.

It is interesting to observe, in passing, that the first beginnings of general international organization were in the form of a judicial body. We have now become quite accustomed to international organizations in all sorts of fields—political, economic, health, transportation, communication, cultural and social—all of which are later in origin than international judicial organization. This is worth remembering when we observe also that the relative development and use of the International Court of Justice now seems to have fallen behind that of the Security Council, the General Assembly, and other branches of international organization.

There was a second Hague Conference which was more notable for what it tried to do than what it actually succeeded in doing. It tried, without success, to create two more permanent tribunals, an International Prize Court and an Arbitral Court of Justice. The United States delegation proposed a true permanent court.

In 1920 a tribunal was initiated which would be both permanent in duration and judicial in character. This was the Permanent Court of International Justice, created in the Covenant of the League of Nations. It was a genuine court, prepared to accept and decide cases under international law as they arose. Although Americans played a large part in leading the way toward these judicial institutions, the United States never became a member of the Court, just as it abstained from membership in the League of Nations. Although President after President urged acceptance of membership, the United States Senate insisted on a number of reservations, beginning in 1926. By 1929, principally through the efforts of Elihu Root, the other nations were persuaded to amend the Court's Statute to grant all the concessions demanded by the Senate. Then, after a lapse of six more years, the Senate refused to approve membership anyway.

Another interesting sidelight on the relation of the United States to the Permanent Court of International Justice is that, except for a few months, throughout the history of that court there was a distinguished American jurist on the bench. There was no requirement in the Statute of the Permanent Court of International Justice that a judge must be a national of a country which was a member of the Court. The four Americans who served as judges were: John Bassett Moore, Charles Evans Hughes, Frank B. Kellogg, and Manley O. Hudson.

Even at this point in the story it can be seen that the role of the United States has been a strangely schizophrenic one. Through the Jay Treaties, through the pioneering work of Elihu Root and others in conceiving and bringing to reality the early international tribunals, not to mention the part played by Woodrow Wilson in the creation of the League of Nations, the United States appeared as the source of constructive ideas in the field of peaceful legal settlement of disputes. The American dele-gations to both the 1899 and 1907 conferences were instructed to press for the creation of tribunals that were ahead of their times. Yet, again and again, when the time came for the United States actually to adopt the creature which its own people had helped so greatly to bring into being, the United States, usually as a result of failure to muster the necessary two-thirds majority in the Senate, repudiated its own brainchild.

All this gave rise to a wisecrack in Europe which went as follows: "The United States gave two things to the world, the League of Nations and cocktails, and then promptly proceeded to deprive itself of the use of both."

In fairness to the American people generally, it should be pointed out that, because of the way in which treaties are made under the Constitution, requiring a two-thirds vote of the Senate in addition to the will of the Executive, it is possible in effect for American foreign policy to be made by a minority consisting of one-third of a quorum of the Senators plus one. Thus, in 1897, a compulsory treaty of arbitration with Great Britain was defeated when the Senators voted as follows: 43 for, 26 against—with 46 needed to carry. The final Senate vote which killed American World Court membership was 52 for and 36 against. Since 59 votes were needed for the two-thirds majority, the consent to ratification was defeated. A fail-ure to approve a treaty or an international organization does not necessarily result simply in absence of foreign policy; it may in itself constitute a definite foreign policy. Thus, although the Constitution contemplates that the

President with the advice and consent of the Senate shall be in charge of conducting foreign affairs, the net result is that one-sixteenth of the members of Congress can in fact make foreign policy. These Senators may represent as little as 6 per cent of the population.

The Permanent Court of International Justice decided sixty-five contested cases between 1922 and the outbreak of World War II and gave twenty-seven advisory opinions. Among the cases it handled were some of first-line importance. For example, it handled a long-standing dispute between Norway and Denmark on the ownership of East Greenland. If anyone is inclined to minimize the importance of the kind of disputes the international courts have handled, he would do well to try to imagine the emotions of the Norwegians on losing this territory which every Norwegian child knows was discovered by Leif the Lucky.

The work of the Permanent Court of International Justice was suspended by the Second World War, and it went out of existence when the League of Nations was dissolved. It was replaced by the present International Court of Justice.

# (12)
# Present World Law
# Machinery

THE PRESENT INTERNATIONAL COURT OF
Justice is essentially a continuation of the Permanent
Court. Its nature, rules, and procedures are largely unchanged. Perhaps the most conspicuous differences are
the membership of the United States and the Soviet
Union in the present Court and the making of the Court
an integral part of the United Nations.

It will simplify understanding the relation of particular
countries to the Court to observe that there are two stages
in a country's relation to the Court. The first is mere
membership. All members of the United Nations are
automatically members of the Court. This membership
in itself does not mean very much, beyond perhaps con-
ferring the right to bring cases in the Court without
any special permission. As noted in the case of the Permanent Court, it is perfectly possible to have a judge on
the Court from a country which is not a member of the
Court, although in the case of the International Court of
Justice this has not yet happened. The important fact is
that membership does not in itself constitute a submission
to the Court's jurisdiction. This requires a second step,
which is the filing of a voluntary acceptance of the
Court's obligatory jurisdiction. Such a declaration may be
unqualified, or it may contain certain permitted condi-

tions and exceptions. At the present time, thirty-nine countries have filed such declarations, some of them containing various reservations limiting the scope of the acceptance. This entire problem of acceptance of the Court's jurisdiction will be discussed in detail in Part Three of this book.

In addition, members may submit disputes to the Court by special agreement on a case-by-case basis. Jurisdiction may also be conferred in advance by clauses in treaties stating that disputes about the particular treaty shall be referred to the International Court of Justice. The basis for jurisdiction in past cases decided by the International Court has been as follows: compulsory jurisdiction under declarations, nine cases; special agreements, four cases; compulsory jurisdiction under treaties, one case; combination of special agreements and compulsory jurisdiction, two cases.

Under the Court's Statute, when a nation accepts the Court's jurisdiction in advance by filing a declaration, it must be limited to "legal disputes" concerning: "(a) the interpretation of a treaty; (b) any question of international law; (c) the existence of any fact which, if established, would constitute a breach of an international obligation; (d) the nature or extent of the reparation to be made for the breach of an international obligation."

A few examples of the kinds of cases brought to the International Court may help to give some idea of the range of disputes that come within the everyday work of the Court. One familiar category of cases is that of disputes over territory and boundaries. Examples would include the long-standing Honduras-Nicaragua boundary dispute decided in November, 1960, and the dispute between France and the United Kingdom over the islands of Minquiers and Ecrehos in the English Channel. Disputes over the rights of nationals in other countries are exemplified by the case between France and the United States concerning the rights of nationals of the United States in Morocco, and a case between France and Egypt concerning the protection of French nationals in Egypt. Other typical cases have included: disputes over fisheries, such as the Fisheries case (*United Kingdom* v. *Norway*) involving disputed fishing grounds off the coast of Norway; disputes over interference with rights of passage of ships, such as the Corfu Channel cases (*United Kingdom* v. *Albania*); disputes over nationalization of foreign-owned industries or investments, such as Anglo-Iranian Oil Company case (*United Kingdom* v. *Iran*); disputes over aerial incidents, such as the cases which the United States attempted to bring against Hungary, Czechoslovakia, Bulgaria, and the Soviet Union as the result of the shooting down of planes; disputes over business, property, or financial rights of nations, individuals, or corporations, such as the case of certain Norwegian loans (*France* v. *Norway*), the case of the monetary gold removed from Rome in 1943 (*Italy* v. *France, United Kingdom, and United States of America*) involving ownership of a large quantity of gold removed by the Germans from Rome in 1943, and the Interhandel case (*Switzerland* v. *United States of America*) involving a controversy between the United States and Switzerland over ownership and control of the General Aniline and Film Corporation.

By special procedures, nonmembers of the United Na-

tions can become members of the Court. Switzerland,
Liechtenstein, and San Marino have become members
under these procedures.

The basic problem, so far as international judicial
machinery is concerned, is that of getting all justiciable
international disputes, both large and small, submitted to
the International Court or some other appropriate tribunal. This problem in turn has two aspects. First, every
effort must be made to find ways of improving and diversifying the machinery of international justice to adapt it
to the kinds of demands that would be made on it under a
true system of international rule of law. In other words,
the prospects of acceptance of international judicial machinery can be and should, as far as possible, be improved
by identifying and making any changes that would make
the Court more convenient, attractive, and usable in the
opinion of the member nations all over the world. This
phase of the problem will be discussed in the succeeding
chapter. The second aspect is that of obtaining acceptance
of the International Court and other methods of pacific
settlement through the creation of real understanding of
and confidence in the processes of international justice.
This problem will be the subject of Part Three of this
book.

As we face up to the question of how to bring about the
optimum structure of international adjudication, we again
find that there are two possible approaches. One is to
construct an idealized blueprint of what such a structure
ought to look like, if we could have unlimited freedom
to amend the Charter of the United Nations and the
Statute of the International Court. This job has already

been admirably done in a book entitled *World Peace Through World Law* (1960) by Grenville Clark and Louis Sohn.

The other approach is to assume that, for the time being, there probably will not be any substantial revisions of the United Nations Charter or the International Court's Statute and then to try to find every conceivable way in which a judicial structure of optimum usability and acceptability can be extracted from the present Charter and Statute by making the most of the rather flexible and broad provisions under which the Court is now organized. The two approaches are by no means inconsistent. Indeed, the second approach is probably the most promising avenue by which the nations of the world may ultimately come to accept the more far-reaching changes contemplated by the first approach.

# (13)
# Attaining the Optimum International Judicial System

THE MAIN STRESS HERE WILL BE ON WAYS of improving international judicial machinery without assuming amendments of the United Nations Charter or the International Court's Statute. There is a practical reason for this. Although it was contemplated that there should be a consideration of Charter revision after the first ten years of experience with the United Nations, this Charter revision process has been repeatedly put off. There appears to be no prospect of change in this situation for some time to come. The reason seems to be that, while every nation can make up a substantial list of changes it would like to see made, it is by no means sure that the final changes might not make things worse rather than better. This feeling was heightened when Khrushchev in the autumn of 1960 proposed radical changes, such as the substitution of a triumvirate for the Secretary-General, which many thought would virtually paralyze the United Nations. The United Nations has indeed been changing rapidly, but the change has been brought about by events and accepted practices rather than by formal amendments of the Charter. We have seen such developments as the remarkable growth of the authority and effectiveness of the Secretary-General's office; the institution and use of the United Nations force in Korea, Gaza, and the Congo; the relative strengthening of the role of the General Assembly in spite of its technical inability to make binding decisions in matters of peace and security; and the transformations brought about by the vast increase in the number of new nations. Perhaps the ability of the United Nations to adapt itself to changing conditions without Charter revision is one of the reasons that formal Charter revision does not receive much support.

The first question which might be posed on possibilities for improvements without Charter revision is whether there is any way in which the composition and staffing of the Court would be bettered within its present framework.

In the last analysis, the quality of the men who serve as judges is more important than any technical or structural provision.

The Court's Statute, in its description of standards to be met by the judges, could probably not be greatly improved on, for it requires that the judges must be chosen from among persons who "possess the qualifications required in their respective countries for appointment to the highest judicial offices, or are jurisconsults of recognized competence in international law."

It is generally agreed among authorities on the subject that these high standards have in fact been observed in practice. Judgeships on the International Court have always been considered a great honor and have been filled by a succession of the most distinguished judges, international law scholars, and high legal officers from various countries. The following capsulized summaries of the backgrounds of the judges will give some idea of their experience and background:

*Dr. Ricardo J. Alfaro* (Panama): President of Panama, Minister of Justice, legal author, chairman of International Law Commission.

*Dr. Abdel Hamid Badawi* (United Arab Republic): Roman and Islamic Law scholar, author of numerous books on international law.

*Dr. Jules Basdevant* (France): Professor of International Law, author of various legal works, legal adviser to Ministry of Foreign Affairs.

*Dr. Jose Luis Bustamente y Rivero* (Peru): President of Peru, Professor of Law, author of several legal works.

*Roberto Córdova* (Mexico): member of International Law Commission, legal counselor of embassy, Washington.

*Sir Gerald Fitzmaurice* (United Kingdom): legal adviser to the Foreign Office, member of International Law Commission, author of several legal works including *The Law and Procedure of the International Court of Justice.*

*Dr. Phillip C. Jessup* (United States of America): ambassador to the United Nations, lawyer, author of numerous legal works, Professor of International Law.

*Dr. V. K. Wellington Koo* (China): Prime Minister, president of League of Nations Council.

*Dr. Vladmir M. Koretsky* (Union of Soviet Socialist Republics): Professor of Legal History and International Law, member of International Law Commission, author of various legal works.

*Dr. L. M. Moreno Quintana* (Argentina): judge in Civil and Commercial Courts of Argentina, Professor of International Law, author of various legal works.

*Dr. M. Gaetano Morelli* (Italy): Professor of International Law, co-editor of the *Revista di diritto internazionale* and the *Trattato di diritto internazionale,* author of numerous legal works, legal adviser to the Ministry for Foreign Affairs.

*Sir Percy C. Spender* (Australia): lawyer, cabinet member, ambassador to the United States, legal author.

*Dr. Jean Spiropoulos* (Greece): Professor of International Law, member of International Law Commission, legal adviser to Ministry of Foreign Affairs.

*Dr. Paul Kotaro Tanaka* (Japan): Chief Justice of the Supreme Court, Dean and Professor of Law of Tokyo University, author of various legal works.

*Dr. Bohdan Winiarski* (Poland): Dean, University of Poznan Law School and Professor of International Law.

If there is any change to be made in the composition of the Court, it would not seem to be a change in the quality and experience of the judges that is necessary. Questions may be raised, however, about the adequacy of the representation of various legal systems or geographical areas. Here again, the actual Statute of the International Court seems to be satisfactory, since it provides in Article 9 that "in the body as a whole the representation of the main forms of civilization and of the principal legal systems of the world should be assured."

If any adjustment needs to be made in this respect, then, it would require simply a selection of more widely representative judges during the regular election process.

The present composition of the Court by continents is as follows:

(1) *Europe* (6)
    Basdevant (France)
    Fitzmaurice (UK)
    Koretsky (USSR)
    Morelli (Italy)
    Spiropoulos (Greece)
    Winiarski (Poland)
(2) *South America* (3)
    Alfaro (Panama)
    Bustamente y Rivero (Peru)
    Moreno Quintana (Argentina)
(3) *Asia* (2)
    Tanaka (Japan)
    Wellington Koo (China)
(4) *Africa* (1)
    Badawi (UAR)

(5) *North America* (2)
   Córdova (Mexico)
   Jessup (USA)
(6) *Australia* (1)
   Spender (Australia)

Another way to group the judges geographically is by certain familiar regional groupings, which would produce the following breakdown:

(1) *Latin America* (4)
   Alfaro (Panama)
   Bustamente y Rivero (Peru)
   Córdova (Mexico)
   Moreno Quintana (Argentina)
(2) *Western Europe* (3)
   Basdevant (France)
   Fitzmaurice (UK)
   Morelli (Italy)
(3) *Eastern Europe* (2)
   Koretsky (USSR)
   Winiarski (Poland)
(4) *Middle East—including the Balkans* (2)
   Badawi (UAR)
   Spiropoulos (Greece)
(5) *Central Asia* (1)
   Wellington Koo (China)
(6) *Eastern Asia* (1)
   Tanaka (Japan)
(7) *North America* (1)
   Jessup (USA)
(8) *Australia* (1)
   Spender (Australia)

    (9) *Southeast and South Asia* (0)
    (10) *African Mid-Continent* (0)

The other relevant grouping is by principal legal systems, which comes out as follows:

    (1) *Roman or Civil law* (7)
        Alfaro (Panama)
        Basdevant (France)
        Bustamente y Rivero (Peru)
        Córdova (Mexico)
        Moreno Quintana (Argentina)
        Morelli (Italy)
        Spiropoulos (Greece)
    (2) *Common law* (3)
        Fitzmaurice (UK)
        Jessup (USA)
        Spender (Australia)
    (3) *Communist law* (2)
        Koretsky (USSR)
        Winiarski (Poland)
    (4) *Islamic law* (1)
        Badawi (UAR)
    (5) *Chinese law* (1)
        Wellington Koo (China)
    (6) *Japanese law* (1)
        Tanaka (Japan)
    (7) *Hindu law* (0)
    (8) *African tribal law* (0)
    (9) *Jewish law* (0)

This last list presents a gross oversimplification but may serve to give a rough idea of the distribution by legal systems. Many of the judges are versed in two or more systems. For example, Judge Wellington Koo has been a student of civil and common law as well as of Chinese law.

In any event, this list of areas and legal systems seems to point up several conclusions. Roman (civil) law seems clearly to be overrepresented at the expense of other legal systems. As to regions, Latin America seems to be too heavily represented, by comparison with Africa and Asia. With the growing importance of continental Africa in world affairs, its lack of membership on the Court, both as a regional and as a legal-system matter, is conspicuous. There is a judge from the United Arab Republic, part of which is in Africa. But there is no representation of the vast portion of the continent which is generally thought of as more characteristically Africa, that is, the nations lying south of the Arab nations on the Mediterranean.

The present International Court is more widely representative than was the Permanent Court of International Justice, which was heavily European in composition. On the other hand, there seems to have developed a sort of unwritten allocation of places on the Court between regions and legal systems which has not varied substantially in recent years. Thus, when a vacancy has been created by death, replacement has usually been from the same area.

The need to adjust the various proportions within the Court may gradually be taken care of in the course of the election process. It will be recalled that, under this process, the candidate for a judgeship must receive a majority both in the Security Council and in the General Assembly.

One result of this arrangement is that the five nations which are permanent members of the Security Council are assured of having a national on the Court. This result is an intentional one and is generally conceded to be essential to the success of the Court. However, for the remaining places on the bench it certainly would not be surprising, in view of the rapidly growing voting strength of the Afro-Asian nations in the General Assembly, to find some correction in the present lack of judges from that area.

Although one sometimes speaks of the legal systems, the areas, or even the countries "represented" on the Court, this word "represented" should not be allowed to create the wrong impression. Apart from the initial effort to insure that there is a reasonable distribution between systems and areas, and apart from the rule that no nation may have more than one judge on the Court, both in theory and in practice the judges act as individuals. As we have seen, they can even be elected from countries that are not members of the Court. Moreover, while their particular legal background is of some interest, once they are on the International Court, it is their function to apply international law, and this is a branch of law which is uniform for all the members and in which they are all experts. One additional concession to "representation" of nations is made in the *ad hoc* judge practice. If a party to a case is a nation which does not have a national on the Court, it is entitled to have an additional judge appointed to the Court at its request for the purposes of that one case. It is interesting, however, that in six out of eighteen instances the *ad hoc* judge has not been a national of the litigant country but has been a distinguished international law authority from some other country. In view of the fact that there are only 15 judgeships and 101 members of the Court, this *ad hoc* judge procedure is probably a justifiable concession to the realities of international life. It is certainly much better than the proposal that the Court should be greatly enlarged so that many more nations could be "represented" on it. This proposal, besides being based on the unsound premise that the judges "represent" their countries, has the vice that it would both make the Court unwieldy and create the implication that the judges were expected to take their country's national point of view.

Thus it may be concluded, at this point, that it is quite possible and desirable to make some gradual adjustment in the composition of the Court by region and legal system and that there is no urgent need for structural or constitutional changes in the process of selection.

Some criticism has been directed at the selection process as involving too great a political element. However the political element has probably been reduced as far as it can be in an international organization such as the United Nations. The original nominations are submitted by national groups. These groups are made up of individuals who are members of the Permanent Court of Arbitration. Countries not represented on the Permanent Court make up a special national group for this purpose. Before they make their nominations, the national groups are required to consult the highest courts, the law schools, the legal profession, and the appropriate legal academies and associations of their countries. As a result, even before the election process begins, the nominating process has gone a long way toward insuring that the selection must be made from a panel of highly qualified candidates. The final test of the validity of the selection system is the caliber of the judges actually chosen, and by this test the present method must be considered largely successful. Of course no system and no human organization is without its flaws. It is well known that there have been several times when international jurists of outstanding distinction have failed of election. There have also been one or two instances in which judges have been elected to the Court whose unorthodox conceptions of international law have caused considerable consternation. But in this respect the International Court is certainly no different from domestic courts, including the Supreme Court of the United States.

Another main line of possible improvement of the International Court takes the form of increasing its flexibility, accessibility, and adaptability to a wide range of demands. In connection with the suggestions which are to follow, it should be remembered that there is a sort of reciprocal relationship between the amount of business brought to the Court and the process of diversifying the Court. At the moment critics could perhaps say that it is no use to talk about contriving arrangements which will enable the Court to handle a much larger volume and variety of cases, since it hardly has enough cases to keep it busy as it is. The answer is that the "world rule of law" movement assumes efforts to make progress on all fronts simultaneously. Therefore, if the world's judicial structure is revised to make it more easy and attractive to bring cases to the Court, the greater volume of cases will begin to appear. We cannot wait for the demand to appear first, because the demand itself is stifled in part by some of the inadequacies of the machinery. We should move forward with plans to devise every possible means of enabling the judicial system to handle the volume and variety of cases it ought to handle under a well-developed system of international rule of law.

A number of interesting proposals have been put forward on how the international judicial machinery could be elaborated to produce the kind of variety of courts and tribunals that we take for granted on the domestic scene. Among these proposals is usually the suggestion that there ought to be a series of regional courts below the International Court. One reason would be the obvious geographical convenience of having courts located in various parts of the world. Another advantage would be that regional courts, staffed by people from the region, would be more apt to command the confidence of people of that region than would distant courts manned by representatives of all cultures.

To increase convenience still further, there should perhaps be traveling courts which would bring the courtroom to all parts of the world. This question of sheer geographical accessibility can be a factor in determining whether the Court is used or not. The tradition of "riding circuit" is an ancient one and seems to be of unusual relevance on the international scene where distance can still be an important factor, particularly to smaller and more remote countries.

Another suggestion has been that the International Court of Justice might be designated a court of appeal on international law questions from the domestic courts of various countries. A branch of the Court sitting in New

York to give advisory opinions to the United Nations has been suggested. There might also be clerks of the Court with convenient offices located at different points around the world to make it easier to initiate and handle a case.

To what extent can some of these suggestions be accomplished or approximated by measures that do not require revision of the United Nations Charter or the International Court Statute? Fortunately there seem to be several provisions of the Court's Statute of such broad scope and flexibility that it may be possible to create, within the present constitutional structure, most of the desired features that have been mentioned.

Although the Court has always sat at The Hague, it is already entitled under its Statute to sit anywhere in the world. It has simply not as yet found it convenient or important to do so. For a start, then, we have all the authority needed for making the Court itself accessible geographically, even to the extent of having it ride circuit.

However, there are obvious disadvantages in having the entire Court attempt this kind of mobility. At this point Article 26 of the Statute of the Court is of interest:

*1.* The Court may from time to time form one or more chambers, composed of three or more judges as the Court may determine, for dealing with particular categories of cases; for example, labor cases and cases related to transit and communications.

*2.* The Court may at any time form a chamber for dealing with a particular case. The number of judges to constitute such a chamber shall be determined by the Court with the approval of the parties.

*3.* Cases shall be heard and determined by the chambers provided for in this article if the parties so request.

Under this article it would seem to be possible to designate a specific panel of three judges drawn from a particular region to hold court in that region and handle cases arising between countries located in that part of the world. Thus something of the practical effect of the regional court could be obtained within the present Statute.

Another article of the Statute with interesting possibilities is Article 50, which states: "The Court may, at any time, entrust any individual, body, bureau, commission, or other organization that it may select, with the task of carrying out any enquiry or giving an expert opinion."

Anyone who is familiar with the workings of modern administrative law in practice will recognize the extensive possibilities opened up by this article. The proportion of everyday controversies which finally culminate in a formal court decision is extremely small. In many areas of law there are various kinds of preliminary procedure involving the finding of facts by examiners, referees, assessors, or masters, sometimes accompanied by an expert opinion on the merits of the case. It frequently happens that, when the matter has reached this stage, it is as good as concluded. One reason is that the factual controversy is often so large a part of the case that the mere settling of the factual questions is almost equivalent to a decision of the case. Another reason is that a litigant, confronted with strong and well-documented opinion adverse to him at this level, may well conclude that it is not worth his while to pursue the litigation further. And so, if we were to assume a large volume of business coming to the

International Court, it could within its present Statute set up as elaborate and permanent a hierarchy of fact-finding and opinion-rendering bodies as the volume and nature of the business would warrant. Here again, the practical effect of a series of lower tribunals could be approximated, even though the lower bodies would not be in a position to give a final legal judgment.

Let us try out this approach on a specific example of a possible new tribunal and procedure that might be of crucial importance in the years ahead: the special problem of interpretation and dispute-settling under any disarmament treaty that might be agreed on. If such a treaty is to be workable and survive, there will have to be a systematic and efficient mechanism designated for disposing promptly of the inevitable disputes on interpretation that will arise. A moment's reflection will show that this dispute-settling mechanism will necessarily have to be of a judicial character. It cannot be an administrative commission, since such a commission would normally be staffed by evenly balanced representatives who would expect to represent a particular interest and who would presumably deadlock on all matters of conflict of interest.

The logical place to look for performance of this interpretation and dispute-settling function is, of course, the International Court of Justice. However, there might be anticipated some reluctance on the part of the Communist nations to accept the full Court, since only two of the fifteen judges are from Communist nations. This difficulty might be met by using the authority of Article 26 to constitute a special three-man or five-man panel, since within the present constitution and membership of the

Court it should be quite possible to arrive at a panel which would be acceptable to all parties. This panel could have the final power of interpretation and dispute-settling under the disarmament treaty. But since the volume of cases might be quite large, this panel could then, using Article 50, set up a regular system of referees who would, by authoritative fact-finding and the preparation of opinions, probably dispose of the great majority of complaints.

Since speed will be of the essence in this class of cases, it may also be observed that the Court already has full authority to take quick and summary action. Article 41 of the Court's Statute provides: "The Court shall have the power to indicate, if it considers that circumstances so require, any provisional measures which ought to be taken to preserve the respective rights of either party."

This provision has been elaborated in the rules of the Court. Article 61 of the rules says that such cases shall be "treated as a matter of urgency." Under this article the Court could issue the equivalent of a cease-and-desist order or a temporary injunction to stop any alleged violation in its tracks pending a more complete hearing on the merits.

This is just a sampling of possibilities for finding variety and flexibility within the present constitutional framework of the Court.

There are several possible features of an optimum world judicial structure which might, under our assumption of no Charter revision, have to take place outside the framework of the International Court. One of the problems most urgently in need of solution, if we are to have rule of law on the international scale, is that of making suitable international tribunals available to private parties. The present unavailability of such courts is a problem of considerable dimension. For one thing, it results in a vast amount of simple injustice. There are literally thousands of claims of individuals and corporations against foreign governments that are gathering dust in the chancelleries of the world because there is no tribunal to which they can be taken as of right. The problem also has a bearing on the question of peace and war, since some of the great international controversies threatening the peace take the legal form of disputes between private parties and governments. The expropriation of the Anglo-Iranian Oil Company and the nationalization of the Suez Canal Company were technically wrongs to private companies.

In one sense there may be said to be a solution within the present Court framework. A state may decide to champion the rights of the individual or corporation before the International Court and may appear as plaintiff. The main trouble here is simply that it leaves the private party completely at the mercy of the discretion of his foreign office on whether the right will be vindicated. If relations between the two countries are bad, the foreign office may tell the individual that it is inadvisable to exacerbate relations. If relations between the two countries are good, the foreign office may say that it would be a shame to disturb these good relations by launching a lawsuit.

There is no way to get the private party into the International Court as of right without an amendment of the Court's Statute. The Statute says point-blank that only states may be parties. In this case, therefore, it would probably be necessary to set up a separate system of international claims courts. This could be done by agreement between as many nations as are interested.

There is ample and encouraging precedent for this procedure in the success of the court of the European Economic Community. This is a special court, unrelated to the United Nations or to the International Court of Justice and open to private parties as well as governments, which handles all disputes arising out of the activities of the various components within the European Economic Community. Its conspicuously successful record during its brief period of existence provides ample evidence that there is no inherent reason why a special court of this kind, open to private parties, cannot be devised to handle a broader area and a broader category of claims.

Of course, just as the court of the European Economic Community was set up by multilateral agreement between the countries affected, so any group of countries that wanted to do so could create a regional court system among themselves by the simple device of a multilateral agreement. Indeed, the same agreement could provide that a final appeal would lie from the decision of the regional court to the International Court of Justice. In this way, again, the benefits of the regional court system could be achieved and brought within the International Court orbit, all without the necessity for United Nations Charter amendment. Some such regional arrangements have been discussed for such groupings as the British Commonwealth countries, the NATO countries, the Arab countries, and the American republics.

However, in all these discussions of possible regional arrangements, it would be most unfortunate if the regional arrangement were thought of as something to be adopted in place of, rather than in addition to, the full use of the International Court of Justice.

Up to this point the discussion has stressed judicial mechanisms. In addition, a complete dispute-settling system for international disagreements should ideally include other tribunals capable of handling matters containing various mixtures or degrees of justiciability and nonjusticiability. Arbitration, as noted earlier, is an ancient, tested, and flexible device, under which parties may prescribe a decision according to law or may prescribe a full settlement of all the issues in a case under principles of justice and equity. Even if full acceptance of the jurisdiction of the International Court were achieved, many of the more important international disputes could not be finally settled in this forum, since they may involve quasi-political claims or since existing legal rules or remedies may be inadequate or inappropriate. An arbitration tribunal, charged with deciding all the issues in a case, would have the necessary competence to deal with such cases. With this kind of problem in mind, some commentators have advanced such ideas as that of compulsory arbitration of "nonlegal" disputes and that of a true permanent court of arbitration which might or might not be given compulsory jurisdiction. Such a tribunal is sometimes referred to as an "Equity Tribunal." (The present Permanent Court of Arbitration, as already noted, is not so much a court as a panel from which parties who want to create a board of arbitrators can make their selection.) The International Court of Justice is now empowered to decide a case *ex aequo et bono* (on equity and justice) if both parties agree, but it is doubtful that this incidental power is an adequate answer to the need for regularized arbitration. To round out the range of tribunals, there should be added the possibility of creating mediation and conciliation bodies to help solve disputes that lend themselves to neither adjudication nor arbitration. Various kinds of mediation devices have been resorted to in recent years in critical situations and have succeeded in bringing about cease-fires and staving off hostilities in some cases, notably the Palestine situation.

It is readily conceivable that, if present efforts to increase use of the international judiciary have some success, mediation and conciliation might also enter on a new and significant role in peaceful settlement procedures. A decision based on law, while clarifying legal issues, may not suffice to solve a claim which demands a change in the legal situation—in other words, which is "political." In such situations the procedures of mediation and conciliation, in which third parties enter into the case with attempts to clear up the issues and with offers of compromise suggestions, may be the most effective means of reaching acceptable solutions. Ongoing commissions and tribunals, available on a regular basis to perform these functions, should be considered as the logical complement to judicial and arbitral bodies in an over-all optimum dispute-settling system.

# PART THREE

# Acceptance of World Law

🔲🔲🔲🔲🔲🔲🔲🔲🔲🔲🔲🔲🔲🔲🔲🔲🔲🔲🔲🔲🔲🔲🔲

## (14)
## Can Nations Accept World Law?

NOW SAY WE HAVE A WORKABLE BODY OF world law, and say we have a working system of tribunals —what good are they if nobody will use them? This brings us to our third requisite of world rule of law: acceptance of the system by the nations affected.

The most direct test of acceptance of world rule of law is the degree to which a nation has accepted the compulsory jurisdiction of the International Court of Justice. Since this test exposes most of the arguments that apply to other elements of world legal order, much of the ensuing discussion will be cast in terms of this issue as it presents itself to various parts of the world. But this procedure should not be allowed to blur the fact that acceptance of world law involves not just acceptance of one

97

court but acceptance of the entire range of items discussed in this book under the headings of substance, machinery, and enforcement of law.

The discussion of the acceptance problem will be
treated under the following headings: in this and the following chapter, an analysis of two matters that are of
equal cogency in all parts of the world—the question of
"loss of sovereignty" and the overriding question of the
contribution that acceptance of world law can make to
peace; then, in the three following chapters, a separate
analysis for three groups of countries—the United States
and similar democracies, the newly developing countries,
and the Communist countries. While all the impediments
to acceptance may be present in all these countries, each
group seems to have its own principal brand of worry or
misunderstanding which holds it back. Roughly, the
main problem of acceptance by groups of countries may
be summarized thus:

*The United States and similar democracies*—a failure to
understand the potential contribution of world law to peace,
and a lingering isolationism or chauvinism which expressed
itself as underestimation of the ability, integrity, and self-
restraint of a tribunal manned by judges from varied legal
cultures.

*The newly developing countries*—a failure to appreciate
the potential contribution of rule of law in hastening economic development, and a mistaken idea that, while they
want change, the law is somehow the guardian of the status
quo and is incapable of accommodating itself to change.

*The Communist countries*—a failure to realize that peaceful coexistence and disarmament cannot succeed without sys-

tematic provisions for settling disputes impartially under law, and an ideological block in the form of viewing the state as the supreme source of law, and law and courts as being within rather than above the over-all pattern of world struggle.

# (15)
# Does World Law Mean "Loss of Sovereignty"?

LET US LOOK AT ONE ARGUMENT THAT IS universal: the argument that acceptance of world court jurisdiction may involve "loss of sovereignty."

Sometimes people in a particular country like the United States seem to think that theirs is the only nation worried about "giving up sovereignty" by accepting world court jurisdiction, as if somehow the particular country had thus suffered a unique loss which has no counterpart in other countries. The fact is that every country is jealous of its sovereignty. Indeed, the newest countries are the most jealous of all. There appears to be a deep-seated law of nature which decrees that the younger a modern nation is, the more nationalistic it is. The older nations gradually have come to wear their sovereignty easily and loosely. Centuries of suffering from nationalistic wars have mellowed their attitude toward "sovereignty" and made them less frantically neurotic about supposed threats to it. They become capable of

such moves as the various supra-national activities undertaken within the European Economic Community, including a court with compulsory jurisdiction over disputes
growing out of Community transactions. By contrast, the
many new nations are sensing the heady thrill of independence for the first time. Inevitably they go through a
period of years during which they proclaim and defend
their "sovereignty" with fanatical ferocity. They are a
little unsure of themselves—and sometimes not without
reason. Events in the Congo showed that the location and
distribution of sovereignty among various political en-
tities may not be securely settled on the country's official
Independence Day.

However, even among the newer countries, after the
passage of only a few years, this excessive preoccupation
with national sovereignty begins to give way to a more
relaxed and confident attitude, assuming the country's
development is reasonably satisfactory. But it is still true
that in every country—young, old or middle-aged—the
cry of "loss of sovereignty" invariably rises when submission of disputes to the World Court is at issue.

One approach to this difficulty has already been urged
in Chapter 6: the presentation of evidence that, under the
legal traditions of practically all societies, sovereignty is
conceived as being under the law and not above the
law. But there is another and simpler point that should be
made whenever this issue is raised. The assertion that
submission of international disputes to a World Court is a
sacrifice of sovereignty is an outright misuse of the term
"sovereignty." It is a rhetorical cliché with proved dema-
gogic appeal. But it will not stand up on analysis.

Here is the reason: International disputes involve the rights of *two* sovereign countries, Country A and Country B. Country A has sovereignty within its own jurisdiction and over rights within that jurisdiction. *But Country A does not have sovereignty over Country B's rights*—and B's rights are involved in the dispute just as much as A's.

Suppose that the United States has a treaty under which American citizens are granted certain privileges within Country B. Suppose a dispute arises in which the United States alleges that these privileges were denied in a particular case. If the United States submits this question to the World Court, has it forfeited its sovereignty? What "sovereignty" did the United States have to make Country B take an action it did not want to take within its own borders?

What really happens when a country accepts international adjudication is not that it diminishes its sovereignty but that it uses its sovereignty to obtain something of value. In the loose use of the term one could just as well say that a nation loses some of its sovereignty every time it makes a treaty. It would be nearer the truth to say that the country *uses* its sovereignty by putting it to work to obtain values that can be secured in no other way. If a country has only one major product, such as coffee, and would also like to have automobiles, refrigerators, and shoes, it will probably make an international trade agreement. In so doing it will give up its sovereign right to bar the entrance of those automobiles, refrigerators, and shoes into its territory. In return it will gain the privilege of sending its coffee into the territory of another country— which until then had the sovereign right to turn the coffee back from its borders. It never occurs to anyone to characterize all this as a "sacrifice of sovereignty."

Similarly, if nations *use* their sovereignty to create an efficient dispute-settling mechanism, they will have used their power to gain something of value—something indeed that is of much greater value than automobiles, refrigerators, shoes, and coffee. Let us now examine the extent of this potential gain by analyzing the degree to which legal dispute-settling could make a contribution to peace.

# (16)
# Justiciable Questions and World Peace

IF NATIONS ACCEPTED SETTLEMENT OF legal disputes under law, the world would gain a substantial advance toward peace.

At the beginning of the book a quick answer was supplied to the familiar question: are the disputes that threaten peace justiciable, or are they political? The answer was that most such disputes nowadays are justiciable in whole or in part. Since this is such a widely misunderstood point, and so essential to the thesis of this book, this answer is now supplemented with more details and examples.

In doing this, we must begin by distinguishing actual active disputes from generalized tension and unpleasantness between states. Strain and struggle, suspicion and exasperation, internal disorder in such emerging countries as the Congo must for our purposes be taken as given quantities on the international scene. Our main concern is, while of course doing everything possible to alleviate them, to keep them from breaking into international violence and war. We are concerned with the question, not whether the parties are willing to submit these disputes today to judicial settlement, but whether the questions themselves are of a quality that is inherently suitable to adjudication. In other words, it is important for the direction of our future efforts to know whether the problem is "can't" or "won't." If it is "can't," our efforts to build peace through law could better be directed elsewhere. If it is "won't," our efforts should be redoubled until "won't" becomes "will."

## Berlin

Of all current disputes, that over Berlin is the most persistent and dangerous. It is easy to fall into the error of thinking of the Berlin problem as a sort of big amorphous bundle of tension. In reality there are at least six clearly identifiable legal issues at the core of the dispute. They are:

(1) The extent of the obligation, if any, of the USSR to permit German personnel and goods traffic between West Germany and West Berlin under the Protocol of

1944 on "Greater Berlin" and the Jessup-Malik Agreement of 1949;

(2) The extent of the obligation, if any, of the Soviet Union to permit Allied military (a) rail, (b) motor vehicle, or (c) air communications between West Germany and West Berlin under

(i) an alleged agreement by Presidential correspondence, acceptance by action or estoppel in 1945,

(ii) an alleged agreement by practice,

(iii) an alleged agreement by incorporation into technical day-to-day agreements in *Kommandatura* committees, especially the Committee on Air Travel;

(3) The extent of the obligation, if any, of the Soviet Union to permit the Western Allies to communicate between West Germany and West Berlin under an alleged rule of customary international law such as easement by necessity;

(4) The right, if any, of the USSR to transfer the execution of its obligations, if any, under the above headings to the German Democratic Republic without divesting itself of its own liabilities to the Western Allies;

(5) The right, if any, of the Soviet Union to divest itself of these alleged obligations completely by according the German Democratic Republic "full" sovereignty;

(6) The obligations, if any, of the German Democratic Republic in either of the two preceding cases. It may be of interest to note that the Soviet Union (un-

like the German Democratic Republic) is apparently not arguing what would be another legal issue, the question whether the quadripartite agreements have been frustrated and rendered obsolete by subsequent events. The reason seems to be that the USSR places strong reliance on the Potsdam Agreement, which was almost contemporaneous with the quadripartite agreement.

If the statements of Khrushchev on Berlin are examined carefully, they will be found to contain many statements of legal conclusions. Thus, as to item (5) above, he said at Baku in 1960 that if the Soviet Union accorded full recognition to East Germany, Western rights of access to Berlin would be lost. Note that this is a statement, not of a political or diplomatic argument, but of an opinion on international law.

As stressed at the beginning of the book, it is not here contended that the authoritative settlement of these legal questions would end the Berlin crisis—but it would help. As matters now stand, the argument swirls around claims of existing legal rights and demands for changes in existing legal rights without distinguishing between the two. Would it not help, for example, to get an authentic decision on the point asserted by Khrushchev and find out once and for all what the *present* legal rights of the Soviet Union are, and its *present* power under international law to transfer its treaty obligations to East Germany? Let these questions, at least, be put to rest and become a firm legal foundation on which diplomatic negotiations about the future of Berlin can be built, instead of on the shifting sands of controversy about present legal rights. In much the same way the International Court of Justice in

1960 decided the legal issues in the politically controversial Goa dispute between India and Portugal, and the
political problem now seems nearer to solution.

### Suez Nationalization

Since Korea the world has probably never been
brought closer to World War III than it was at the time
of the British-French-Israeli invasion of Suez. The dispute
over the nationalization of the Universal Suez Canal Company was originally and essentially a justiciable question
of international law. To anyone who is inclined to say that
the justiciable questions are not the big ones threatening
peace, the Suez conflict could stand as a virtually complete answer in itself.

Two agreements were involved: the agreement between Egypt and the Universal Suez Canal Company,
which still had a number of years to run, and the Convention of Constantinople of 1888, which had a large
number of seafaring nations as signatories and which laid
down the rules guaranteeing freedom of passage through
the canal.

It is known that the British considered trying to take
the Suez nationalization to the International Court. It is
not known why they decided against this move and resorted to gunboats and bombing planes instead. Of course,
it is quite possible that the court approach would not have
worked, for jurisdictional or other reasons. When a similar episode was unfolding in Iran, in the form of seizure
of the Anglo-Iranian Oil Company by Mossadegh, Britain
did take the case to the Court. Ultimately the Court found
that it could not take jurisdiction over the merits of the

case, but in the meantime the very presence of the case in Court while temporary measures were being attempted helped to keep that dispute from exploding into general war. Why the British did not pursue a similar course in respect to Suez remains a tragic mystery.

There is another Suez problem that is both older and newer. This is the dispute over the actions of the United Arab Republic in asserting belligerent rights against Israeli ships and against cargoes destined for or coming from Israel, desiring to transit the canal. In spite of efforts of the United Nations and a resolution of the Security Council calling on Egypt to desist from interfering with canal traffic, this problem has become more acute as the United Arab Republic has detained ships and seized cargoes in recent years.

Throughout the ten years that this controversy has been under discussion, it has been consistently recognized as involving a question of international law by all parties. The first sentence of the note of Israel to the president of the Security Council in 1951 asking that the case be placed on the agenda states: "In contravention of international law, of the Suez Canal Convention (1888) and of the Egyptian-Israel general armistice agreement, the government of Egypt continues to detain, visit, and search ships seeking to pass through the Suez Canal, on the grounds that their cargoes are destined for Israel . . ."

This being so, in view of Article 36(3) of the United Nations Charter which states that legal disputes should normally be referred by the parties to the International Court, one might have expected a referral to the International Court sometime during the ten years.

What actually happened? The admitted legal questions

were simply bypassed, under the leadership of the United Kingdom, the United States, and France, in a resolution passed by the Security Council finding Egypt at fault and calling on her to desist from the practices complained of. The United Kingdom representative, speaking on behalf of the three cosponsoring powers, said: ". . . these legal issues are no doubt debatable, but I do not consider that it is necessary for the Security Council to go into them. . . . The view which the Council takes on this question should depend, in our opinion, on the actual situation as it exists rather than on any legal technicalities." The objections to this brushing aside of the legal issues came from Egypt, as a party in interest, and from Nationalist China and India.

It is too obvious for discussion that the central issues here are justiciable in quality, as has been conceded by all the countries involved. There are such familiar questions as the law concerning contraband, visit and search, blockade, the belligerent status of parties, the effect on the alleged state of "war" of the Armistice of 1949, and the effect of the outbreak of hostilities in 1956 on the Armistice of 1949.

It is sometimes said, or implied, that one obstacle in the path of international rule of law is that some other parts of the world do not share or understand our conception of law. The present case may be a salutary corrective to any undue resort to this excuse. It is interesting here that it was India and China that were on the side of giving respect to legal rights. It is particularly ironic that they were demonstrating this devotion to law in connection with a body of law which was the peculiar creation of European and American countries, i.e., contra-band, blockade, visit and search, etc.—a body of law which, far from rejecting as alien, they understood per-fectly and insisted on having applied.

It is still not too late to take this dispute to the Court. The Secretary-General urged this as recently as 1959. But Israel—and this is a commentary on what happens when the judicial function is usurped by a political organ —declined to go to Court on the ground that the Se-curity Council action had disposed of the case. It may be objected that Egypt would never consent to a suit by Israel, especially since Israel was of course not a party to the Convention of Constantinople of 1888. But, as in the earlier Suez case, this is no excuse for not trying. Refusal to accept suit would put Egypt's position in an entirely different light in the eyes of such countries as India and China, which insisted that the legal approach be used first. In any event, since Egypt has accepted the com-pulsory jurisdiction of the Court on questions under the Convention of Constantinople in relation to parties to that treaty, surely a suit could be brought by a party, such as Denmark, when one of its Israeli-bound ships is stopped.

Once more the conclusion is clear: the factor that is keeping this case out of court is not inherent nonjusticia-bility; it is voluntary choice.

### Sino-Indian Border

Another dispute occupying the front page from time to time is the Sino-Indian border dispute. Both parties here are claiming certain border territories and both ar claiming as of legal right. The rules of law applicable to the settlement of boundary disputes are rather limited, since ordinary common sense and logic places a limit on the number of ways in which boundaries are established and claims to territory made good. There appears to be no real misunderstanding between communist and noncommunist countries on what their criteria are. In this case the issues are numerous and vary from segment to segment of the frontier, but they include whether there are in some cases boundaries agreed on by the parties or their predecessors in interest and whether in some places effective control has been established by one or the other party up to the boundary claimed. These are eminently justiciable issues. The issues are examined in a thirty-page article in the January 1960 issue of the *International and Comparative Law Quarterly* by Alfred P. Rubin. All reports are that the attempts of Chou and Nehru to work out a settlement have failed. After looking at this thirty-page article and trying to imagine Chou and Nehru struggling with each one of the complex portions of this controversy, one cannot be surprised at this failure. One can feel only compassion for the negotiators.

Boundary disputes generally are amenable to judicial and arbitral handling. They have supplied a large fraction of the subject matter of international dispute-settling under law. The notable Jay Treaty, leading to the arbitration of the Maine–Nova Scotia boundary after the Revolutionary War, has already been discussed in Chapter 11. Perhaps one of the finest examples of entrusting really large territorial disputes to adjudication was the litigation in the Permanent Court of International Justice between Norway and Denmark over the ownership of East Greenland. Norway lost and accepted what must have been a crushing blow with good grace.

Although this case involved a huge amount of territory, it is not the amount of real estate involved that makes boundary disputes explosive. It is the patriotic and emotional impact of the loss of a portion of the sacred soil of the homeland. Was there ever a more inflammatory or bellicose presidential campaign slogan than "54:40 or fight"? In the closing scene of Hamlet, with the protagonists all lying dead on the stage, Fortinbras speaks of battles over land which hardly contains room to bury the dead. Incidentally, he seemed to be referring particularly to the Scandinavian countries—the very countries that in this century let a Court decide between them as to the huge territory of East Greenland.

The World Court has handled a number of boundary and territorial disputes and decided another late in 1960 —the Honduras-Nicaragua dispute which had been festering for half a century or more.

## Aqaba

Another Middle Eastern dispute which has threatened to precipitate war and may do so again is the controversy over rights of passage through the Gulf of Aqaba and Straits of Tiran. At bottom, this is almost purely a legal dispute. Indeed it presents the international lawyer with an entire symposium of questions of law. Does the gulf "comprehend international waters"? To what extent is the gulf part of the coastal states' territories? To what extent is the gulf a historic international bay? To what extent is the gulf a series of territorial seas? To what extent historically is the gulf an Arab gulf without any international character?

If the gulf comprehends international waters, to what extent do the laws of war apply to the gulf and to the Straits of Tiran? What is the law applicable to the straits? Does it include Article 17(4) of the Convention on the Territorial Sea and the Contiguous Sea of the Geneva Conference? Are the laws of war in force since the adoption of the United Nations Charter, and if so, are they applicable to Israeli or Israeli-bound ships? To what extent is there a "war" between Arab states and Israel? Was the so-called war legal? If not, is reliance on the laws of war admissible? Has the Armistice of 1949 ended the "war" and thus rendered irrelevant any of the laws of war? Has the 1956 fighting affected the 1949 Armistice? Even if war continues, what are the rules applicable to innocent passage anywhere? In the gulf? Through the straits? To what extent is the right of innocent passage restricted by the "rights of protection of the coastal state"? If there is no war between the Arab states and Israel, to what extent is the relevant Israeli-bound traffic not "innocent passage"?

Here again, both sides are grounding their claims on rights under international law.

## Refugees

The refugee problem must be listed in any catalog of current festering sources of tension, particularly the Arab refugee problem.

Some of the legal questions would be these: Did the refugees leave voluntarily or involuntarily? Were they forced to leave by violence or terror? Have they a right to return? Have the original legal rights and duties now been made obsolete and incapable of implementation by continued Jewish immigration to Israel? If the Arab refugees do have continuing rights, can these be satisfied by payment of damages?

Again, if these legal questions were cleared up, perhaps we could make more progress on the difficult political problems surrounding the plight of refugees.

## Aerial Incidents

With the effects of the U–2 and RB–47 incidents still apparent, it requires no argument to show that aerial incidents are a major source of international tension. Characteristically they are the kind of disputes that a Court is well equipped to handle. Indeed, the United States has had seven cases of this kind on the International Court's "General List"—numbers 22, 23, 25, 28, 36, 40, and 44. Usually the primary question is one of fact, as in the RB–47 case: was the plane actually over the territory of the country which shot it down? Then there may be subsidiary questions of the right to shoot down the plane in any event and of the treatment of the passengers and crew.

People often ask: would you really want the U–2 case to go to Court? The answer is that if the United States could have all aerial cases go to court—those in which our planes were not over the line, those in which they may have strayed a small distance over the line inadvertently, and those in which they were far inside the line as in the U–2 case—the United States would be far ahead, since the cases in which the law was on its side would far outnumber those in which it was legally in the wrong.

### Expropriations

The question of the right of the government to nationalize foreign businesses and of the extent and terms of adequate compensation is a legal question.

The principle is the same as that in the Suez and Anglo-Iranian nationalization cases. Cuba and Indonesia, whose expropriations are only the most recent in the headlines, have not accepted the jurisdiction of the World Court. But this does not change the fact that the disputes created by their nationalizations are legal in quality and, under a fully developed world legal order would ultimately be dealt with by judicial means, if diplomatic settlement failed.

This is just a sampling of current controversies in terms of their suitability for adjudication. Quantitatively, some of them might seem to rank as major issues and some as minor issues. However, in the world's present condition, it is a serious mistake to assume that international controversies can be measured and weighed and assigned a quantitative rating and then to conclude that the danger to peace involved in the controversy is in direct proportion to this quantitative size. The Aqaba dispute is perhaps small in size, but it could very well be the spark that blows up the Middle Eastern powder keg. When the powder keg has blown up, it is not going to matter whether the spark was a big one or a little one. This factor is important when people raise the question whether the movement to strengthen the international rule of law and the judicial settlement of disputes really has a major part to play in averting war and building peace. People who raise this question will sometimes say, in effect, "It is all very well to settle disputes like Aqaba; but if the land armies of the USSR start grinding across Poland and middle Europe, what can these fifteen old men in The Hague do to stop them?" The answer is that this is only one conceivable way that the peace might be seriously broken, and by no means the most likely. It is pointless to try to calculate the relative gravity of those controversies threatening the peace that are capable of final settlement through the judicial process. The important fact is that most disputes threatening the peace are in whole or in part justiciable, and to the extent that these are cleared up by the application of law through judicial or arbitral procedures, the prospects of peace will have been measurably increased.

# (17)

# Acceptance by the United States and Similar Democracies

IN THE UNITED STATES THE ISSUE OF INTER-
national rule of law as represented by the International
Court of Justice has been brought to a sharp focus by the
controversy over repeal of the "Connally Amendment."
The treatment of American acceptance of world law can
therefore be given both timeliness and practicality by
using repeal of the Connally Amendment as a proving
ground. At the same time it will be evident in the course
of the discussion that, while a few of the points raised are
exclusively applicable to the United States and to the
Connally Amendment question, most of the points presented are relevant to the broad question of international
rule of law in all its aspects and are applicable to other
similar democracies.

The United States has deposited a declaration under the
optional clause accepting the Court's jurisdiction, but
with several reservations, one of which is so damaging
that it is generally understood to destroy its acceptance for
all practical purposes. Under this reservation the United
States excludes from its acceptance of the compulsory
jurisdiction of the Court: "Disputes with regard to matters which are essentially within the domestic jurisdiction

of the United States of America *as determined by the United States of America.*"

The Connally Amendment consists of the words "as determined by the United States of America." This is sometimes called the "self-judging clause," because it purports to confer upon the United States the unreviewable power to decide, in a case in which it is an interested party, whether the International Court legally has jurisdiction over the case.

It is significant that the Senate committee which handled this declaration in 1946 considered the question of a self-judging clause in the course of its hearings and deliberately rejected it. It unanimously reported a declaration with no such clause attached. However, the self-judging clause was added in the course of the debate on the floor of the Senate. The debate shows that the self-judging clause came in on a wave of considerable confusion about the facts and the law surrounding this issue. The most serious misunderstanding was the fear that, without the Connally Amendment, the International Court could take jurisdiction over such traditionally domestic matters as tariffs and immigration.

It is important at this point to stress that the issue is not whether the Court should take jurisdiction over domestic questions. Opponents of repeal often talk about the "Connally Reservation" rather than the "Connally Amendment" and then cite the entire domestic jurisdiction reservation as if this were the "Connally Reservation." This creates a misleading impression. The true fact is that, with the Connally Amendment deleted, the United States' declaration would still exclude "disputes with regard to matters which are essentially within the domestic jurisdiction of the United States of America." Indeed, in addition to this continuing explicit reservation in the declaration, there are at least two other specific guarantees that the Court's jurisdiction will be confined to questions of international law. One is Article 2(7) of the United Nations Charter, which states: "Nothing contained in the present Charter shall authorize the United Nations to intervene in matters which are essentially within the domestic jurisdiction of any state or shall require the Members to submit such matters to settlement under the present Charter . . ." Moreover, Article 36(2) of the Statute of the International Court of Justice limits the Court's jurisdiction to "international legal disputes" in four named categories: international treaties, international law questions, breach of international obligations, and remedies for such breach. The Court's jurisdiction is not a sweeping one, limited only by the operation of negative reservations. On the contrary, the Court possesses jurisdiction over areas affirmatively entrusted to it by its Statute, and these areas are confined to the four international categories just named.

The main practical consequence of the Connally Amendment, then, is not to change the boundaries of the Court's jurisdiction, which will be exclusively limited to international law questions whether there is a Connally Amendment or not. The real consequence of the Connally Amendment is to create a two-way veto power over the Court's jurisdiction. First, the United States can prevent adjudication in any case brought against it under the declaration by stating that in the opinion of the United States the matter is essentially within its domestic jurisdiction. Second, because of the principle of reciprocity, any other country can similarly prevent adjudication in any case brought by the United States by stating that in that country's opinion the matter is essentially within its domestic jurisdiction. The authority for the second statement is the case of certain Norwegian loans (*France* v. *Norway*).

## The Arguments for Repeal

When a change is being advocated, it is a fair question to ask: What will be gained by making the change?

The concrete gains, in addition to the gain of an advance toward peace discussed in Chapter 16, can be stated under three main headings:

(1) The right to vindicate American legal rights in circumstances under which the United States could now be thrown out of court under the reciprocity rule;

(2) Freedom from the legal uncertainty, as well as the embarrassment, of trying to operate under a declaration which is apparently invalid;

(3) The right and the ability to assume a position of effective leadership in the promising peace through law program which is now surging forward all over the world.

## Effect of Reciprocity on American Rights

The first gain is one which should prove convincing to the most hardheaded advocate of American self-interest. The United States, by repealing the Connally Amendment, would gain the ability to obtain satisfaction of its legal claims, and those of its citizens and corporations, in the World Court against other countries which can now throw it out of court because of the reciprocal effect of this amendment.

Although a country might state that it would never invoke the reservation except in genuinely domestic cases, there is nothing the United States can do if the reservation is invoked against it even in obviously international disputes. The net effect, therefore, is that the United States can now be blocked in any case whatever that it might attempt to bring against any country under the general jurisdiction of the Court. This is such an important and little-understood fact that it is worth stating again in the bluntest possible terms: The Connally Amendment destroys, by our own act, absolutely and without exception, every conceivable right that the United States might have in any circumstance to enforce any legal claim under the general jurisdiction of the Court against any country on earth. No matter how fully the other country might have accepted the International Court's jurisdiction, under the principle of reciprocity it has only to say, when sued by the United States, "We think this case is domestic," and the United States is out of court without any legal recourse whatever.

The principal authority for this holding of reciprocity is the Norwegian Loans case. In that case, Norway had issued a large quantity of bonds in France payable in gold. Then Norway went off the gold standard and refused to service or pay these bonds in gold. France brought an action on behalf of its citizens in the World Court demanding payment in gold. Norway had accepted the World Court's jurisdiction without reservation. France had a "Connally Amendment" copied from that of the

United States. The Court held that Norway could invoke against France her own self-judging clause on the principle of reciprocity. Norway, therefore, merely stated that in its opinion the question of payments on its bonds issued in France was essentially a domestic Norwegian matter, and France's claim had to be dismissed.

Result: financial loss in cold cash to hundreds of thrifty Frenchmen. Cause: a supposedly protective clause interposed by the supposed guardians of French self-interest. Sequel: France repealed its self-judging clause.

The opponents of repeal of the Connally Amendment have had surprisingly little to say about this vital issue bearing on American self-interest and the rights of American individuals and corporations. The only reply they have advanced which has any legal pretensions is the conjecture that France probably would have lost the case anyway, on a theory that Norway's refusal to pay its bonds in gold in France was indeed a domestic issue. Of course, even if this argument were correct—which it is not—it would be beside the point. The point of the Norwegian Loans case is that it unmistakably established the principle of reciprocity, and no matter who might have won in the case the decision served notice for all future time that the self-judging clause is a boomerang. However, since the legal point has been raised, it is worth pointing out what the rule of international law on this subject really is. In Charles Cheney Hyde's standard treatise, *International Law* (1945), this respected authority sums up the law as follows:

If one may conclude, as does the Supreme Court of the United States, that a bond-issuing State is competent to enter into binding obligations that pledge its credit, it can not modify or destroy them without having recourse to conduct which the State of the obligee may fairly regard as amounting to internationally illegal conduct and as constituting the breach of an international obligation toward itself. Moreover, modification or destruction is believed to be apparent when the obligor State, through the exercise of its sovereign power to regulate the value of money renders it impossible for the alien obligee to enjoy the benefits of payments in the particular currency (such as gold) which it agreed to pay.

In addition, France's case included a contention that Norway was practicing discrimination between bondholders of different countries. This in itself would probably be a breach of international law, apart from any claim of economic necessity for going off the gold standard in relation to other countries generally.

The Norwegian Loans case, moreover, is not the only authority for the reciprocity principle. The Interhandel case (*Switzerland* v. *United States of America*) states: "Reciprocity enables the state which has made the wider acceptance of the jurisdiction of the Court to rely upon the reservations to the acceptance laid down by the other party."

It has sometimes been argued that the self-judging clause is unimportant because it is never invoked. This is the exact opposite of the true fact. Since the Norwegian Loans case called attention to this reservation, the self-judging clause has been invoked either directly or reciprocally in every case in which it was available. There have been three such cases. The first was the Norwegian Loans case itself, in which the reservation was invoked reciprocally. The second was the Interhandel case, in which the United States itself invoked its own self-judging clause as to one of the issues. The third was the case of the aerial incident of July 27th, 1955 (*United States* v. *Bulgaria*). This was a claim brought by the United States arising out of the shooting down of an Israeli plane by Bulgaria, with the result of loss of lives of American passengers. As to the United States, Bulgaria interposed three defenses, of which the second was that Bulgaria was entitled to invoke the Connally Amendment on the basis of reciprocity and that the matters in controversy in the case were essentially within the domestic jurisdiction of the People's Republic of Bulgaria, as determined by the People's Republic of Bulgaria.

The argument is also sometimes made that American individuals and corporations are not threatened with loss because only states can be parties to the proceedings before the International Court. This overlooks the fact that, in a large proportion of cases, the state appears as party of record, while the real party in interest is an individual or a corporation. The state acquires a cause of action because its citizen or corporation has been aggrieved through failure to obtain justice in the local courts. Note that in all the cases just mentioned there were individual or corporate rights at stake: the rights of French investors in the Norwegian Loans case, the ownership of General Aniline and Film Corporation in the Interhandel case, and the compensation of the next of kin of the nine United States citizens killed in the aerial incident in July 27, 1955.

The other principal argument made by opponents of repeal to offset the self-interest argument is that Ameri-

can corporations and individuals would prefer to press
their claims in local courts rather than in the International Court anyway. This misses the point. Of course
local remedies must be pursued first. This is not only
good policy for reasons of local good will; it is indeed
mandatory under international law that local remedies be
exhausted, as has been held most recently in the Interhandel case. But the argument stops short of the main
issue. Once local remedies have been exhausted unsuc-
cessfully, what then?

Once local remedies have been exhausted by American individuals or corporations, the claim becomes that of
the United States. The availability of a final showdown
before an international tribunal will not only undo injustice in the particular cases that come before the tribunal but will also have the effect of raising the standards
of local justice and making resort to the International
Court unnecessary in many cases by decreasing the number of instances of claimed local injustice.

A curious inconsistency in this argument by opponents
of repeal is that in one breath they tell us that judges from
foreign countries—even the outstanding experts chosen
for the International Court—cannot possibly understand
the American concept of justice, and in the next breath
they insist that American corporations and individuals
are happy to entrust their fortunes to whatever judges
might preside over foreign local courts and hence do not
need the ultimate protection of the International Court.

The arguments against this demonstration of American
self-interest, then, are wrong on the law, deeply inconsistent, and ultimately based on the grotesque assertion

that the country whose national, corporate, and individual rights are many times more deeply involved and more subject to possible harm in other countries than those of any potential opponent in court really has no interest in having an authoritative legal forum in which to vindicate those rights. After all, American citizens have 29.7 billions of dollars of direct private investment in other countries. This does not include investment in bases, governmental installations, and public programs such as economic and technical aid. There are almost 500,000 Americans resident abroad, and 730,000 tourists and travelers per year. All these persons and property rights are exposed to both personal and property damage, for which ordinarily a legal claim would be the remedy. As a matter of simple arithmetic, therefore, since the Connally Amendment at one stroke destroys both the right of the United States to sue and its obligation to accept suit, it is clear that the United States loses many times as much as it gains; it has many times the legal interests in need of legal protection.

At this point one may well recall the lines of Robert Frost from his poem "On Mending Wall":

> Before I built a wall I'd ask to know
> What I was walling in or walling out.

A specific application of this self-interest point to a type of case of lively current importance is the protection of American business interests and investments abroad. We have been witnessing a wave of expropriations in such countries as Indonesia and Cuba. These expropriations are only the most conspicuous examples of a problem of interference with foreign business interests, which ranges all the way from outright confiscation to various subtle kinds of discrimination. It is true that neither Cuba nor Indonesia happens to have any declaration accepting the compulsory jurisdiction of the International Court, and consequently the repeal of the Connally Amendment would have no particular effect one way or another on our rights in relation to these countries as long as their position remains unchanged. However, there are at present thirty-nine countries that have declarations in force, and of these only four in addition to the United States have self-judging clauses. These four are Liberia, Mexico, The Sudan, and the Union of South Africa. This leaves thirty-four countries that have made declarations, without self-judging clauses, recognizing the compulsory jurisdiction of the Court. These countries are:

| | |
|---|---|
| Australia | Israel |
| Belgium | Japan |
| Cambodia | Liechtenstein |
| Canada | Luxembourg |
| China (Nationalist) | The Netherlands |
| Colombia | New Zealand |
| Denmark | Nicaragua |
| Dominican Republic | Norway |
| El Salvador | Pakistan |
| Finland | Panama |
| France | Paraguay |
| Haiti | Philippines |
| Honduras | Portugal |
| India | Sweden |

| | |
|---|---|
| Switzerland | United Kingdom of Great |
| Thailand | Britain and Northern |
| Turkey | Ireland |
| United Arab Republic | Uruguay |

The repeal of the Connally Amendment would result in a concrete change and gain in the rights of the United States in relation to these countries. In circumstances under which they now could throw the United States out of court by the reciprocal effect of the Connally Amendment, the United States could hereafter invoke the compulsory jurisdiction of the World Court to vindicate its legal rights, whether as a nation, as corporations, or as individuals.

It is also true that, as to the other countries of the world which have filed no declarations at all including all the Communist countries, the repeal of the Connally Amendment would not affect the rights of the United States one way or the other. That is, its ability to sue a Communist country would be no greater than before. It should be clearly understood that, contrary to some of the implications left by the opponents of repeal, revocation of the Connally Amendment would also not have the slightest effect on the ability of Communist countries to bring the United States into court. Since the Communist countries have not accepted the Court's jurisdiction on any terms, by reciprocity the United States can continue to block any case brought by a Communist country against it if it chooses to do so.

There is one special application of the damage to American self-interest which is so poignant and para-

doxical that it deserves separate mention. When the
United States first went into the economic and technical
aid program, the guardians of American self-interest insisted on reserving the right to have legal claims growing
out of this program adjudicated in an impartial tribunal.
Accordingly, the Economic Cooperation Act of 1948 itself required that a clause be inserted in all economic and
technical aid agreements under which the other country
agrees to accept determination by the World Court or
other tribunal of claims of Americans growing out of economic and technical aid programs. Seventeen treaties
have been concluded under this clause. However, the
Connally Amendment is incorporated by reference in
these treaties, together with its reciprocal effect. The result is that the privilege of requiring impartial adjudication of claims, which this legislation and these agreements attempted to confer on American citizens, has been
wiped out by the Connally Amendment. The repeal of
the Connally Amendment, therefore, would not only restore the general rights of the United States to invoke the
jurisdiction of the International Court but would also restore the specific rights which the Congress so pain-
stakingly attempted to confer on Americans under the
economic and technical aid program.

## Is the Connally Amendment Valid?

The second tangible gain that would flow from the repeal of the Connally Amendment would be to get rid of
both the uncertainty and the embarrassment of having a
declaration which is probably invalid.

Article 36(6) of the Statute of the Court provides: "In the event of a dispute as to whether the Court has jurisdiction, the matter shall be settled by the decision of the Court."

The United States is a party to the Statute and is legally bound by it. While the World Court has not directly passed on the question, seven judges in separate opinions have pronounced the Connally Amendment invalid. The late Sir Hersch Lauterpacht, a member of the Court and one of the world's leading authorities on international law, stated: "An instrument in which a party is entitled to determine the existence of its obligation is not a valid and enforceable instrument of which a court of law can take cognizance." Judge Lauterpacht cited Samuel Williston on *Contracts* (Revised edition, 1936) as authority for this familiar basic principle.

There is nothing worse in law or business than legal uncertainty. If one knows for certain that the law is against him, at least he can start from there and make plans for the future. But if one is in a state of uncertainty, neither a lawyer nor a businessman knows how to conduct his affairs while the uncertainty remains.

Even if we assume that the Connally Amendment is invalid, there is still uncertainty about the effect of the invalidity. Two judges, Lauterpacht and Spender, and other international lawyers and scholars have concluded that the invalidity renders the entire American declaration a nullity. This assertion is made on the ground that, as Lauterpacht stated, it creates a document in which one party determines his obligation and which therefore is not cognizable in law. If this is the correct conclusion, the net result of the Connally Amendment is that the United States finds itself lumped with the USSR and the other countries which have no declaration at all.

Five other judges and authorities have expressed the view that the invalid portion of the declaration is severable. This would result in exactly the opposite effect. The United States would be subject to the compulsory jurisdiction of the Court as if the Connally Amendment did not exist. Out of all this confusion one fact is certain: The United States cannot make its plans for the future with any confidence and will never know the real answer until it either repeals the Connally Amendment or waits until there has been a final adjudication in the International Court, both on the legality of the declaration and the effect of any illegality. It would be a distinct gain simply to remove this uncertainty so that the United States would know where it stands in relation to the International Court.

There would also be a gain in removing the humiliation and embarrassment that attends this self-judging clause because of its flouting of one of the most elementary principles of civilized society: the principle that no man shall be judge in his own case. If any person attempted to assert the right to be judge in his own case in a domestic matter, he would become a laughing stock. The effect is no different on the international scene. If anyone is in any doubt, he has only to attend a few international conferences of lawyers, and he will discover that the Connally Amendment is constantly thrown up to Americans by lawyers from other countries who are bewildered by the spectacle of such a declaration from a country they have come to think of as a fountainhead of the rule of law.

The position of the United States looks particularly bad because the Connally Amendment was the first self-judging clause in the history of International Court jurisdiction. Of course, there have been various kinds of reservations without self-judging clauses, and the Statute of the International Court expressly permits such reservations. But it is wrong to argue, as opponents of repeal argue, that there is no difference between carving out an area by a straightforward reservation, in one case, and asserting the self-judging right in another. If a country, in its declaration, carves out an area, such as a particular boundary or river dispute, no question of legality arises. In such instances the International Court would be the final arbiter of the question whether the case before it fell within the asserted reservation under international law. It is an entirely different matter to claim the self-judging privilege. The reason is that the self-judging provision does not merely carve out one named area of jurisdiction; it gives the claiming country an unreviewable right to make the reserved area as large or as small as it chooses at its own whim. It appears to accept compulsory jurisdiction of the Court with one hand and snatches it away with the other, not in absolute terms, but in terms that are unpredictable and subject to administrative determination by the country after it has become a party to an existing lawsuit.

For example: Suppose I make a contract with you for personal services. You agree to pay me $300 a month for a year. I agree to perform personal services as your employee and to do such jobs as you order me to do. However, I insert a clause in this contract saying that I reserve the right to refuse to perform "domestic services" for you. This would undoubtedly be a valid reservation. If you ordered me to go to your residence and scrub floors for you, and I refused, an impartial tribunal could easily pass on the question whether I had violated my contract of service. But suppose I go on and insert in my reservation a self-judging clause so that, while you are obliged absolutely to pay me $300 a month per year, I have the right to refuse to perform "domestic service as determined and interpreted by me." Would this be a valid contract as it stands? Suppose that every time you ordered me to perform some service I stated, "In my opinion this is domestic service and I refuse to perform." Obviously, one of two results is legally possible. Certainly no court is going to compel you to pay me $300 a month for the privilege of listening to me repeat monotonously, "I declare this service to be domestic." Therefore, either the court will hold the entire agreement invalid, or it will hold the self-judging clause invalid and serverable and take upon itself the normal court function of deciding whether the particular service was or was not domestic. These are the two positions taken by judges and scholars on the American self-judging reservation. It either makes the entire declaration a nullity, or it simply knocks out the self-judging feature and leaves the United States in the position of being subject to the normal compulsory jurisdiction of the Court as if the self-judging clause did not exist.

Therefore, when opponents of repeal say that, in adhering to the self-judging clause, the United States is doing no more than following the policy which this country adopted fifty or more years ago, that is, the policy of accepting the jurisdiction of international tribunals only on a case by case basis, they are missing the essence of the self-judging problem. If the United States wanted to pursue a policy of accepting international adjudication only on a case by case basis, it should simply file no declaration of acceptance of compulsory jurisdiction at all, and this would leave it in precisely that position. In so doing, the United States would declare to all the world that it is going to copy and follow the Russian example so far as the International Court of Justice is concerned and abandon the company of the thirty-eight countries that have declarations.

But certainly it was the intention of this country and of other countries at the time of forming the United Nations and enlarging the membership of the International Court to take a step forward toward settlement of international disputes by peaceful legal means as the normal and regular method. The United Nations Charter makes this clear. The United States did file a declaration. The object of the present move to repeal the Connally Amendment is to make the substance of the action of the United States in accepting International Court jurisdiction live up to its apparent purpose.

### Effect on the Over-All Peace Through Law Program

The third major gain that repeal of the Connally Amendment would bring would be the restoration to the

United States of the ability to undertake a position of leadership in the broad program of achieving peace through law in the world.

Over the past few years a tremendous amount of momentum has been built up for this promising effort. The American Bar Association's Special Committee on Peace Through Law, as discussed in more detail in Chapter 29, has organized four international regional meetings of lawyers for the purpose of stimulating peace through law programs in all countries of the world, and a global meeting at which, with the assistance of the ideas gained at the regional meetings, a world-wide action program to strengthen the substance, the machinery, and the acceptance of law in international affairs will be undertaken. The Special Committee has also built up contacts with dozens of people around the world, has prepared and distributed a wide variety of useful background materials, and has helped to stimulate the creation of over a hundred state, local, and affiliated committees on peace through law, all of which in turn are engaged in action programs to the same end.

In universities, law schools, and research centers there has been a distinct upsurge in research, publication, teaching, and clarification of international law, and a similar trend is observable among top governmental officers, governmental agencies, the United Nations agencies, and voluntary and professional associations.

However, with all this heartening groundswell of activity, there is serious danger that the United States will see its best efforts blighted by the charge that its deeds do not match its words. Here again, anyone who attends in-

ternational conferences or who deals with international
lawyers and officials from other countries is acutely conscious of the ever-present problem of how to answer the
question, which inevitably comes after a discussion of
strengthening international rule of law has been
launched: "That is all very well, but what are you going
to do about the Connally Amendment?" The following
statement by the Indian Ambassador to the United States,
Mahomedali Currim Chagla, who is also a distinguished
judge, is typical of world opinion:

> You will forgive my saying so but I cannot understand how
> the United States can justify a piece of legislation which
> reduces the Court to a mockery and which effectively prevents
> any rule of law ever being established in the international
> field. You must not forget that the United States proudly
> claims to be the leader of the free world. She wants peace
> but peace with justice and how can you ever have justice if
> the only forum which can settle international disputes is
> reduced to a humiliating position where it cannot entertain
> any disputes which ought to be properly decided by it?

When the United States first passed the Connally
Amendment, its lead was followed by seven other countries. The trend is now definitely away from this kind of
clause, but the leadership has been taken by France and
India, which repealed their self-judging clauses in 1959.
Great Britain had one applicable to a different reservation and also abandoned it. The United States is the only
major power retaining the self-judging clause.

Repeal of the Connally Amendment, then, is an important move both in the substantive improvement it
would work in the settlement of international disputes

under law and in the gain which would result in removing the roadblock that is now threatening the peace through law movement in general, and America's prestige and leadership in particular.

## Analysis of Arguments Against Repeal

As against these demonstrable facts showing the gains that would result from repeal of the Connally Amendment, the objections to repeal that have been advanced in various circulars, speeches, and articles over the past few years are strikingly devoid of solid substance. The presentations in favor of the Connally Amendment are largely made up of unsupported fears, inaccurate assertions about international law with no citation of sources, gratuitous suspicions and accusations against the International Court and its members without any reference to the record of either the Court or the individual members, and conjectures about the future performance of the Court and the future nature of international law which assume that individuals, institutions, and even legal systems can overnight turn a 180° angle and become the exact opposite of everything they have been since their inception.

In support of this characterization the arguments against repeal will now be listed, together with the correct facts and law drawn from authoritative sources.

## Guiding Rule of Law for "Domestic" Matters

Opponents of repeal constantly make the unsupported assertion that there is no rule of law to guide the Court in determining what matters are essentially international or domestic. The fact is that the International Court has a clear rule of law which it has laid down on this point. The test is not whether the matter involves more than one country's interests, or geographically transcends national boundaries, or has repercussions in foreign lands. The test is whether the matter is one regulated by international law. This rule was laid down by the Permanent Court of International Justice in its *Nationality Decrees Issued in Tunis and Morocco* opinion and has been the guiding rule ever since: "The words 'solely within the domestic jurisdiction' seem rather to contemplate certain matters which, though they may very closely concern the interests of more than one State, are not, in principle, regulated by international law."

In the teeth of this straightforward rule of law and a straightforward record of its past observance, the opponents of repeal continue to argue that the International Court is somehow going to take over control of vast areas of our domestic life. One of the most widely circulated leaflets, the circular of the "Patriotic Letter Writers, Inc.," which was one of a number of such circulars put out to stimulate a letter-writing campaign prior to the 1960 Senate hearings on the Connally Amendment, actually contained the following statement purporting to summarize the effect of repealing the amendment:

This Court, loaded with members of the Communist Party and their dupes, would have jurisdiction over all areas of our life, for Congress will *no longer* control our—
   trade and tariffs
   civil rights

economics and education
foreign trade
immigration and emigration
International Bank for Reconstruction and Development
mental health and birth control
post offices and censorship
the military
welfare

Another widely circulated newsletter, *The Dan Smoot Report,* added an even more astonishing question: "What if we tried to discontinue foreign aid to some communist or neutralist nation now receiving it, and that nation sued us in the World Court because we were hurting its economy?"

And here is an actual quote from an editorial in the Chicago *American* of February 25, 1960:

If the Connally Amendment were repealed, the World Court could conceivably order the State of California to set Caryl Chessman free, on the ground that putting him to death might stimulate riots in Uruguay, thus disturbing the peace and tranquillity of a foreign nation. The World Court could declare any provision of the United States Constitution invalid if it affected the interests of any foreigner in a way that the Court considered unfavorable. The Court would have the power to destroy all our American institutions.

Of course, none of these allegations ever show the existence of any principle of international law regulating the subject matter which the Court is supposedly going to take over. The writers simply jump to the conclusion that, if a particular matter has any kind of effects abroad, the International Court will grab jurisdiction over it. This is precisely what the International Court has already said that it will not do. It has explicitly said in the *Nationality Decrees* opinion that the mere fact that a certain matter very closely concerns the interests of more than one state is not a reason for its taking jurisdiction. It is difficult to see how the rule could be put in plainer terms. The matter, to come within the Court's jurisdiction, must be one regulated by international law.

In most of the subjects listed in these circulars and editorials there is no conceivable question of regulation by international law. The administration of domestic justice is the clearest kind of domestic question. The discontinuance of foreign aid would be a simple exercise of the most elementary right under international law to make or not to make such international agreements as a nation chooses. The suggestion that such areas as economics and education, mental health and birth control, post offices and censorship, the military and welfare within a particular country are regulated by international law is so patently false that, if comparable statements were sent through the mail about commercial products, they would certainly be considered violations of mail fraud statutes.

There are four areas of domestic policy which have been so frequently brought up that they deserve separate mention. These four are: tariffs, immigration, the Panama Canal, and civil rights.

## Tariff Policy

Ever since Senator Tom Connally first introduced his amendment on the floor of the Senate, supporters of the

Connally Amendment have been making the unsupported assertion that the United States would lose control over its policy of raising or lowering tariffs if the Connally Amendment were repealed.

This charge is not only unsupported but is in direct conflict with the clear and unqualified body of international law on the subject. All authorities uniformly hold that control of tariff policy is a domestic matter. Indeed, there is no record of any state attempting to assert the contrary. It is sometimes easy to forget that every other country is as anxious as the United States, some much more anxious, to keep control over tariff policy. International law on the subject is summed up in the standard treatise, L. Francis Oppenheim on *International Law* (1940), as follows: "Most states have kept up protective duties to exclude or hamper foreign trade in the interest of their home commerce, industry, and agriculture, and, also, their self-sufficiency in the event of war. . . . In thus interfering with the free flow of goods . . . States do not act in contravention of International Law." Perhaps the thing which tends to confuse the opponents of repeal is that a country may, of its own free will, voluntarily make a treaty dealing with tariffs. When it does, to that extent it of course intentionally limits its freedom of action. The interpretation of that treaty, like the interpretation of any treaty, becomes a matter of international law. In such a case it is not the presence or absence of the Connally Amendment or an act of the Court that gives international character to the obligation assumed. It is the deliberate choice of the United States or any other country to grant some concession in order to gain a tariff or trade advantage for itself.

## Immigration Policy

The argument about immigration policy put forward by the opponents of repeal runs closely parallel to the argument about tariffs. The fallacy in the argument, the complete lack of authority supporting it, and the uniform state of international law holding immigration policy to be domestic also closely parallel the tariff situation. Immigration policy, like tariff policy, is exclusively a matter of domestic concern under all cases and authorities, both national and international. Georg Schwarzenberger states: "It is uncontroversial that every State has absolute discretion over the admission of foreigners."

The domestic decisions of various countries are to the same effect. The rule in the United States, for example, is stated in *United States* ex rel. *Knauff* v. *Shaughnessy*: "At the outset we wish to point out that an alien who seeks admission to this country may not do so under any claim of right. Admission of aliens to the United States is a privilege granted by the sovereign United States Government." The law in other countries is the same.

## Panama Canal

The charge that the rights of the United States in the Panama Canal would be endangered by the repeal of the Connally Amendment is, like the other charges, unsupported by law or evidence. The correct fact is that the rights of the United States in relation to Panama would not be damaged or threatened by repeal of the Connally Amendment; on the contrary, the prospects for their protection would be substantially improved.

An analysis of the rights of the United States in relation to the canal falls into two parts: rights in relation to the Republic of Panama and rights in relation to all other countries.

As to the Republic of Panama: the rights of the United States are assured in the United States treaties with Panama of 1903, of 1936, and of 1955. Even if one were to assume the worst and postulate an attack on the original 1903 treaty on the ground of alleged duress, there are a number of reasons, each sufficient in itself, why this poses no hazard under international law. For one thing, in international law duress is not a ground for asserting invalidity of a treaty, even if it existed in this case, which would be problematical. A moment's reflection will show that, if duress invalidated international treaties, there could never be a valid peace treaty.

In any event, once more assuming the worst as to the first point, the basic agreement has been voluntarily re-affirmed by both parties under circumstances where there could be no conceivable claim of duress, in the treaties of 1936 and 1955. This removes any possible doubt concerning the validity of the agreement, under which "The Republic of Panama grants to the United States all the rights, power and authority within the zone mentioned . . . which the United States would possess and exercise if it were the sovereign of the territory . . . to the entire exclusion of the exercise by the Republic of Panama of any such sovereign rights, power or authority."

In the case of *J. N. Gris* v. *The New Panama Canal Company,* the Supreme Court of Panama said: ". . . [T]he Republic of Panama agreed that the United States should possess and exercise, to the entire exclusion of the Republic, those rights, powers and authority, that is to say, the rights, power and authority that a sovereign alone can have."

As to the rights of the United States in relation to other nations of the world, the basic rule is established by a World Court decision, *The SS Wimbledon.* This case holds that a canal connecting two open seas is not deemed subject to an international regime in derogation of the control of the constructing state unless and to the extent that the canal is "permanently dedicated to the use of the whole world." This can only come about by a deliberate act, such as a treaty. The controlling treaty—the Hay-Pauncefote Treaty of 1903—was made with Great Britain and promises that the canal "shall be free and open to vessels of commerce and of war of all nations observing these Rules." This clearly grants a right to Great Britain which the United States is bound to respect. Whether other nations could directly enforce such a right by virtue of a treaty to which they were not a party has never been decided. However, assuming they could, the specific rights so granted to them or to Britain or Panama do not prejudice the essential rights of the United States necessary to its own security. It is now established under customary international law, as the result of accepted practice in relation to this and comparable canals, that in time of war the

United States may deny or restrict passage through the canal to the extent necessary to protect either its defense or its neutrality.

It is clear, then, that the United States has no cause for concern about the reservation of its rights in the Panama Canal. What is less generally understood is that the United States would actually gain a valuable asset for the improvement and protection of its rights in Panama by the repeal of the Connally Amendment. Panama has accepted the compulsory jurisdiction of the International Court without reservation. Panama is therefore one of those countries that, under the reciprocity principle, could now throw the United States out of court under the Connally Amendment by declaring any case essentially domestic.

Suppose, for example, that a number of citizens of Panama somehow managed to seize control of the canal or a part of it. What would the United States do? The supporters of the Connally Amendment might answer that the United States should resort to military action. Yet this is precisely what the United States objected to in the case of the British and French action in Suez. Certainly it would be a disaster for the United States to become maneuvered into a position where the only alternatives available to it were loss of control of the canal or military action to regain it. There is another course open, but it is possible only if the Connally Amendment is repealed. This would be the orderly and civilized course of taking the case to the International Court of Justice. As shown above, the law would be overwhelmingly on the side of the United States in such a case. But as matters now stand,

Panama could merely invoke the reciprocal effect of the Connally Amendment, declare the question to be essentially within the domestic jurisdiction of Panama, and block the United States in legal action.

## Civil Rights

The control of such matters as internal civil rights, school integration, and other human rights matters is so obviously a matter of domestic jurisdiction that the books of international law may be searched in vain for any reference to the subject. Apparently the only reason the subject has arisen is the action of the United Nations in relation to the Universal Declaration of Human Rights and the Draft Covenant on Human Rights. All that needs to be said about these two documents is that they do not create any law, any legal rights, or any legal obligations. So far as the Universal Declaration of Human Rights is concerned, this is elementary. Kelsen, in his standard treatise, *The Law of the United Nations,* states pointblank: ". . . [t]he legal effect of the recommendations made by the General Assembly is . . . that . . . they are not binding."

At the time the Declaration was adopted, Mrs. Franklin D. Roosevelt stated on behalf of the United States: "In giving our approval today to the Declaration, it is of primary importance that we keep clearly in mind the basic character of the document. It is not a treaty; it is not an international agreement. It is not and does not purport to be a statement of law or legal obligations."

The Draft Covenant on Human Rights creates no legal

obligations either generally or in specific relation to the United States. It creates no obligations generally because it was never even adopted by the General Assembly. As for the United States, it has never been signed or ratified by the United States, and the United States has made it clear that it has no intention of signing or ratifying it.

While on this subject, one should probably take the occasion to deal with one of the more fanciful charges made by the opponents of repeal—that individual Americans might be tried criminally by the World Court. The answer to this lies in Article 34 of the Statute of the International Court of Justice, which provides: "Only States may be parties in cases before the Court."

## "No Distinction Between Domestic and Foreign Affairs"

Having been repeatedly challenged over a period of years to come up with some kind of law or authority or documentation for their charges, the opponents of repeal have finally found one isolated sentence in a State Department bulletin: "There is no longer any real distinction between 'domestic' and 'foreign' affairs."

Read in its context, this sentence cannot by any stretch of the imagination be found to have a bearing on international law. The context is indicated by the sentence which immediately follows in the pamphlet:

> Practically everything we do, the way we tax and spend our national income, the way we run our public and private business, the way we settle the differences among ourselves and with other nations, what we say in our newspapers, over the

air and on public platforms, our attitudes toward each other and toward other peoples—all these things affect not only our security and well-being at home, but also our influence abroad.

Americans are constantly being told nowadays that anything that happens at home may have repercussions on the American image abroad. This is true of both our successes and our mistakes. Local strike violence may hurt our prestige abroad, just as conspicuous success in labor relations may improve it. A sensational crime may damage our reputation abroad; a sensational constructive achievement may help it. A highly publicized local scandal may in some degree discredit us internationally; a highly successful cultural or scientific or educational achievement locally will make our stock go up abroad. This has been a major theme for years of those who are trying to make Americans more conscious of their position of world leadership and the responsibilities that go with it.

This is precisely what the State Department pamphlet was dealing with. The most that could be read into the sentence is that almost everything we do may concern the interests of more than one state. But the International Court in its *Nationality Decrees* opinion has said plainly that matters are not removed from domestic jurisdiction merely because they "may very closely concern the interests of more than one State."

The sentence in this State Department pamphlet does not say that there is no longer any difference between matters regulated by international law and matters regulated under domestic jurisdiction. It does not even come close to saying this. As matters now stand, we see the spectacle of one irrelevant sentence from an ephemeral bulletin placed in the scales to counterbalance almost four hundred years of solid international law made up of custom, treaties, diplomatic usage, decisions, and writings of authorities.

## The Court's Record on Domestic Jurisdiction

All authorities agree that the Court has taken a conservative attitude toward its jurisdiction. Perhaps the most striking objective evidence of this attitude is the fact that, of twenty-nine separate contentious matters disposed of by the Court since 1945, the Court has dismissed fourteen on jurisdictional grounds. One of the most outstanding and experienced authorities on international law, now a judge of the International Court, Phillip C. Jessup, made the following statement at the 1960 Senate hearings on the Connally Amendment: "A study of the jurisprudence of the International Court of Justice reveals that . . . the Court has not showed the slightest inclination to amplify its own authority or to act in any but a judicial and impartial way."

Another of America's most eminent international law scholars, Professor Quincy Wright, as part of his statement at the same hearings gave a specific illustration from an International Court decision:

I suggest that domestic jurisdiction—a state has domestic jurisdiction in every dispute whatever, except those in which it has accepted an obligation by treaty or in which it is bound by an obligation under general international law, and I want to point out that the International Court of

Justice has leaned over backward on the question of jurisdiction.

Let me just give an illustration in the case of the Lotus,
which is a case where Turkey was claiming jurisdiction over a
French officer who was accused of having been negligent and,
as a result, had collided with a Turkish vessel on the high
seas, with the resulting loss of lives of several Turkish sea-
men.

Now, France claimed that Turkey had no jurisdiction over
this matter. The International Court of Justice said that
jurisdiction depends on sovereignty; that it belongs to the
state that contests the jurisdiction of a state, to show a positive
rule of international law that imposes an obligation upon
the state in the circumstances.

It found that France was unable to show that Turkey was
bound by any obligation of international law and that, therefore, the matter lay within the domestic jurisdiction of Turkey.

## Attack on Competence of Judges from Other Nations

One of the most unfortunate features of the debate on
the Connally Amendment is that it has led to a number
of gratuitous and uninformed attacks on the competence
and judicial integrity of the judges from other countries
represented on the Court. These attacks and insinuations
are never supported by reference to the actual background, training, or record of any of the present judges, or
by citation of any of their opinions or votes in particular
cases. Many of the attacks consist of little more than the
rather unworthy assumption that lawyers from other parts

of the world with grounding in different legal systems cannot possibly understand basic concepts of law and justice.

The actual record of the backgrounds and experiences of the judges plainly demonstrates that this is one of the most distinguished and competent courts in the world. The qualifications of the present judges are given earlier in Chapter 13.

Having for several years been confronted with this factual record and having been repeatedly challenged to bring forward some evidence to support their attacks, the opponents of repeal have finally produced one such attempt. It occurs in Loyd Wright's dissent to the report of the Special Committee on World Peace Through Law. In this dissent Wright cites an obituary of Judge Alejandro Alvarez in a London paper. Alvarez was a judge of the International Court until about six years ago. The obituary mentioned that Judge Alvarez took quite a broad view of the power of the judge to change the law and believed that law was ultimately related to politics.

The appraisal of Judge Alvarez' reputation represented by this obituary is factually correct. This is something that international lawyers and scholars have known for many years, just as an occasional judge will be found in domestic courts who takes an unorthodox view of the judicial function. But here, once again, the citation proves the opposite of the point intended. For one thing, in order to find an individual for specific attack, the opponents of repeal continue to disregard all the present members of the Court and have to direct their fire at a man who has not only been off the Court for six years but who is also dead. More significantly Wright overlooks the fact that the very obituary which he cites as authority states that the unorthodox views of Judge Alvarez actually set him apart from his colleagues. The obituary says: "His opinions . . . were highly individual. . . . [H]e was prepared to take—indeed could not be restrained from taking—a bolder line than his colleagues." The net effect of the obituary, therefore, is not to support the conclusion which Wright draws—that all the members of the Court are suspect—but rather to prove the opposite, that the other members of the Court were quite unlike Judge Alvarez.

So far as the quality and integrity of the Court's decisions are concerned it is generally agreed that they are excellent. Of course, it is always possible to disagree with particular decisions, and it is difficult to apply objective standards to the performance of any court. However, the World Rule of Law Center at Duke University has made an exhaustive analysis over a period of two years of all the individual votes and opinions of the judges of the International Court of Justice and has reached the conclusion that there is no noticeable difference in their votes or opinions on particular issues attributable to differences in the legal systems of the judges' countries. The allegation that these judges cannot understand fundamental concepts of law and justice is refuted by such an analysis. Indeed, the writer has throughout this Connally Amendment debate been challenging the opponents of repeal to take a blindfold test—that is, read the opinions and votes of the various judges without knowing which judge is the author and then attempt to identify which opinions and votes are those of Islamic, common law, civil law, Communist, Chinese, or other judges. The challenge has never been accepted. The study referred to indicates that such a blindfold test would quickly explode the myth that these distinguished judges cannot be trusted because of their divergent legal backgrounds.

## Judicial Integrity

It is sometimes alleged or implied that judges on the International Court will act as politicians rather than as judges and will vote according to national interest and party line. This implication can be refuted by objective evidence from the record. The record shows that judges from different countries have voted against the position of their own countries in a remarkable proportion of cases. To get the actual figures on this point, the 53 separate issues have been examined on which judges have voted when their own countries were parties in cases before the International Court of Justice. These 53 separate issues have resulted in 103 known votes by these "national judges." (This is because there are usually two national judges, one on each side, voting on each issue, and in addition there happened to be one case in which the dispute was among four countries; five of the total 108 such votes are unknown.)

The significant fact is that the national judge voted against the position advocated by his own country in 24 of 103 votes. This means that the national judges have voted against their own countries' contentions in almost one-fourth of all occasions to vote, because the judge thought his own country was wrong on the law. Even in those cases when a national judge voted for his own country's position, he was with the majority of the Court 43 out of the 79 times, and consequently the vote could hardly be necessarily attributed to considerations other than the merits. On eleven of the occasions in which a national judge voted against his country's position, other judges on the Court voted in favor of that position.

## The Judges from Communist Countries

Some of the more extreme opponents of repeal of the Connally Amendment have tried to make much of the fact that there are two judges from Communist countries on the Court. This leaves the Court with a thirteen to two majority of non-Communist over Communist countries. Somehow the extremists manage to convert even this one-sided lineup into a Communist-dominated Court. The circular of the Patriotic Letter Writers, Inc., cited earlier, may be recalled, which stated that the Court is "loaded with members of the Communist Party and their dupes."

It would not be difficult to imagine that the Communist countries might be somewhat unhappy about the ratio between Communist and non-Communist countries whose nationals are on the Court. But it is harder to understand why opponents of repeal are afraid of the Court because it has two nationals of Communist countries out of fifteen judges.

In addition, a study of the complete record shows no evidence of any distinctive Communist party line in the votes of the judges from Communist countries. Judge Winiarski of Poland has voted with the majority thirty-three times and with the minority five times. Combining the votes of two successive judges from the Soviet Union, S. B. Krylov and F. I. Kojevnikov, we find the Soviet judge has voted with the majority twenty-two times and with the minority thirteen times. The next earlier judge from a Communist country, Milovan Zoričić of Yugoslavia, whose term expired in 1958, voted with the majority twenty-six times and with the minority four times. There are more than fifteen instances in which the votes of judges from Communist countries have contradicted one another. In the only case involving a Communist country in which the International Court has acquired jurisdiction, the Corfu Channel case in the *Merits* judgment, three judges from Communist countries, Zoričić, Winiarski, and Judge *ad hoc* Bohuslav Ečer, voted against a Communist country, Albania, and in favor of Great Britain, on one of four issues decided by the Court. In a recent case involving the United States, the Interhandel case (*Switzerland* v. *United States of America*), the Soviet judge, Kojevnikov, voted in favor of the United States position in three of five issues decided by the Court. On one of these issues the United States judge, Green H. Hackworth, voted against the United States position, while Kojevnikov voted for it.

### The Fear of Future Change

When an examination of the present law, the present facts, and the present composition of the Court has been completed and found to contain no support for the position of the Connally Amendment defenders, they fall back upon the argument that, regardless of the present state of affairs, there is always the danger that the Court and the law may change.

As to a change in the Court, we have a matter of simple arithmetic. The judges hold office for nine years. Five judges are elected each three years. Any change sufficient to alter the character of a majority of the fifteen judges would thus take at least six years. The present declaration of the United States is terminable on six months' notice. Of course, this kind of change is simply not going to happen as a matter of realistic fact. No such change has been perceptible in the last forty years. The judges are elected according to an elaborate procedure designed to bring forward the finest possible judges and to preserve the standards and traditions of the Court. It is fantastic to suppose that suddenly this same procedure is going to produce wild-eyed, fanatical politicians on the bench who are committed to a conspiracy to injure the United States. Late in 1960 six new judges were elected. Once more the selection system brought forward an outstanding group of the world's most distinguished and competent international lawyers and jurists.

However, although no radical change in the Court's attitude is forseeable and although the present state of international law poses no threats to American interest, there is still encountered the last-ditch argument that international law itself may change from its present position to one which would be harmful to the United States. This contention betrays an elementary misconception of the sources and nature of international law.

Changes in international law that affect the United States cannot generally come about against its will. The two major sources of change are treaties and practice. As to treaties, no treaty binding the United States can be changed or created without its consent.

As to practice and customary international law, in view of the dominant place occupied by the United States in international affairs and practices, a practice or custom rejected by the United States would not be considered to be one generally acquiesced in by states. And as to a particular or regional custom relied on by a party, the International Court has said in the Asylum case (*Colombia* v. *Peru*): "But even if it could be supposed that such a custom existed between certain Latin-American States only, it could not be invoked against Peru which, far from having by its attitude adhered to it, has, on the contrary, repudiated it by refraining from ratifying the Montevideo Conventions."

The arguments that have been presented so far constitute the main points that involve the facts and law about the relation of the United States to the International Court. Several miscellaneous arguments may also be briefly touched on.

## Is Military Strength Enough?

One of these arguments is that the United States does not really need the Court because it is militarily strong and can always rely on its power to protect its rights. This conception is out of date. There may have been a time when, if an Englishman's hat was knocked off in Rangoon, the British Navy moved in. Two developments have not only changed this situation but actually reversed it. The one development is the outlawing of force in international affairs except in self-defense and authorized collective action. The other is the building up of force so devastating that it simply cannot be used in the situations where force was once relied on. It used to be that the small and weak countries were the most eager to rely on international law, because it was one way in which to offset superior military power. The situation now seems to be reversed. The great powers, for all their military might, are so muscle-bound by unusable power that they find themselves standing helplessly by while smaller nations expropriate their investments, abuse their citizens, and carry on all kinds of belligerent and abusive activities. The attempted British-French action in the Suez was considered by practically everyone to be an anachronistic throwback to a past era, and the action of the United States and of the United Nations in demanding cessation of the Suez action put an end once and for all to this means of protecting national rights. The net result is that the great powers, with their many interests in other countries in need of protection, are realistically more in need of a working system of adjudication than any other countries, to protect themselves from the tyranny of the weak.

## World Government

Occasionally the opponents of repeal will say that repealing the Connally Amendment implies favoring world government. This is not true. Repealing the Connally Amendment would affect only the judicial side of international activity and would do so not by changing the nature of the Court but by increasing the effectual use that the United States could make of it. The legislative or executive side of international activity would remain unaffected.

## Voluntary Restraint in Use of Self-Judging Clause

It has sometimes been argued that the Connally Amendment is not really objectionable because the United States would never invoke it except in bona fide cases of genuinely domestic jurisdiction.

There are several answers to this rather naive argument. The first is that, even if the United States makes this assertion, it cannot realistically expect all the other countries of the world to take its word for the assertion. To the other countries of the world the Connally Amendment stands as an outright veto power. The question whether it was invoked in improper cases could never really be settled anyway, because the invocation of the self-judging clause is not subject to review by any impartial tribunal.

In the most recent case involving the self-judging clause, the Interhandel case, the United States invoked the domestic jurisdiction reservation under circumstances which brought criticism not only from people in other countries but from many leading American authorities in international law. Without going into the merits of this particular use of the Connally Amendment, one is on solid ground in stating that there are many people in the world who would cite this as one instance of an improper use of the self-judging clause. This is as far as one can go, since the decision is, under present circumstances, unreviewable.

A more practical objection to this argument is the fact that, even if the United States could assume that it would never use the reservation except in proper cases, it has by reciprocity handed thirty-three other countries the power to invoke the reservation against the United States. Are Americans also sure that these other thirty-three countries will never invoke the reservation except in proper cases? In view of the deep suspicions of foreign concepts of justice that pervade the arguments of the opponents of repeal, it is a safe assumption that they would make no such statement. This merely underlines the fact that, if the United States is not prepared to concede this amount of infallibility to the thirty-three other countries, it can hardly expect them to concede this amount of infallibility to the United States.

There is one final argument that weakens the suggestion of taking the United States restraint in the use of the self-judging clause as a matter of faith. The defenders of the Connally Amendment have themselves discredited their own position on this point by their attempts to push the self-judging principle too far. When the Geneva Conventions on the Law of the Sea were before the Senate for advice and consent to ratification on May 26, 1960, the Senate refused to approve the Optional Protocol referring disputes of interpretation to the World Court unless a Connally Amendment was attached. Now the

Conventions on the Law of the Sea are by definition international treaties, and the interpretation of an international treaty is by definition a matter of international law. The Senate action, backed to a considerable degree by the opponents of repeal of the Connally Amendment, thus in effect demands the right to declare issues to be domestic which are by definition matters of international law. How then can the defenders of the Connally Amendment seriously contend that they are only interested in having the United States reserve from the International Court's jurisdiction those questions that are clearly and purely domestic? What answer do they have when people from other countries ask, "If you say you would invoke the Connally Amendment only in genuinely domestic matters, why do you insist on inserting it into exclusively international treaties such as the Conventions on the International Law of the Sea?"

Thus it is that extreme advocates of a position will sometimes damage their case by trying to carry it too far. It reminds one of a statement made in one of A. P. Herbert's fictitious *Misleading Cases* (4th edition, 1928) at page 36, the case of *Rex* v. *Haddock*. The judge, who thought that the defendant had made one argument too many, characterized the argument as follows: "It is like the thirteenth stroke of a crazy clock, which not only is itself discredited but casts a shade of doubt over all previous assertions."

## Is American Opinion Ready for This Move?

A final argument sometimes heard is that, whatever the intrinsic merits of the case for repeal of the Connally Amendment, the American public is not yet ready for such a move. This assertion is belied by objective facts contained in two public opinion polls.

The first was a poll taken by Elmo Roper and Associates, dated September, 1959, of leaders in the legal profession (all members of the American Bar Association House of Delegates plus presidents of all state and major local bar associations). It showed the following response to Question 4:

(a) I believe we should modify the U. S. reservation and leave it to the International Court of Justice to decide whether a particular dispute is within the domestic jurisdiction of the U. S. ..........................67%

(b) I do not believe we should modify this reservation ..........................19%

(c) I have not reached a decision on this matter . 14%

A poll of nationwide cross section consisting of 1,050 prominent Americans listed in *Who's Who* and 244 persons from selected occupations, taken by Columbia University Bureau of Applied Social Research in 1959, asked whether the United States should accept compulsory jurisdiction of the Court in relation to named groups of countries—if these countries were willing to do the same. The response was "yes," by a simple majority in the case of communist countries, by a three-to-one majority in the case of NATO countries, and by a two-to-one majority in the case of other countries.

This, then, is a comprehensive checklist of the arguments that have been made against repeal of the Connally Amendment. Their uniform lack of substance on

analysis impels one to recall the words of Ralph Waldo
Emerson: "It is the duty of the scholar always to declare that a popgun is a popgun, though the ancient and
honorable of the world affirm it to be the crack of doom."

As indicated at the outset, much of the substance of
the arguments here reviewed has relevance to the attitude
of other democracies toward the Court. Why, for example, at the time of the nationalization of the Universal
Suez Canal Company by Egypt, did not Great Britain take
the case to the International Court of Justice? One of the
reasons seems to have been a sort of general distrust, of
the kind discussed in this chapter, of a Court made up of
judges drawn from various legal systems other than that
of the common law. It is hoped, therefore, that the evidence drawn from these new studies of the record of
the Court will help not merely to eliminate such an obvious obstacle to progress as the Connally Amendment
but also to remind all the democracies that they can resort to this tribunal with confidence in its judicial quality
and its high legal competence.

# (18)

# Acceptance by the Newly Developing Nations

OF THE MORE THAN ONE HUNDRED NA-
tions in the world, thirty-nine have filed some kind of

declaration recognizing the compulsory jurisdiction of the International Court of Justice. Of these, ten are from Asia: Cambodia, Nationalist China, India, Israel, Japan, Pakistan, Thailand, Turkey, and so much of the United Arab Republic as is located in Asia. From Africa there are only four: Liberia, The Sudan, the Union of South Africa, and the Egyptian portion of the United Arab Republic. From Latin America there are Colombia, Dominican Republic, El Salvador, Haiti, Honduras, Mexico, Nicaragua, Panama, Paraguay, and Uruguay, for a total of ten.

Some twenty of the newer nations have scarcely had time to think about such matters as filing World Court declarations. Nevertheless, the relatively smaller proportion of declarations compared with that of the non-Communist countries of Europe naturally leads to the question whether there are any special reasons why this should be so. The question is particularly important with regard to the African countries, where the degree of acceptance is the smallest.

One of the reasons has been mentioned in an earlier chapter. It is the feeling that international law as it has developed in the past is not really their law but is a remnant from an earlier era from which they are trying to break away. As has already been suggested, there are several approaches to this problem, including a deliberate attempt to infuse international law generally with a much larger content of "the general principles of law recognized by civilized nations" and an accelerated effort to blanket troublesome areas of international law with multilateral treaties. In both cases, by the very nature of the source of the principles and law, the acceptability of the system will be assured. It has also been indicated that greater representation by the newer nations, particularly of Africa, on the International Court would be justifiable and desirable.

Another reason for this relative coolness toward law may be the curious reversal, already mentioned, between the positions of the weak nations and strong nations. In earlier years the law was the best defense of the weak against the strong. Today, although the nuclear powers are relatively much stronger by comparison with the weaker nations than ever before, the outlawing of force in international affairs has made all this power relatively useless in the everyday problem of protecting national interests. There is a rather poignant paradox here. Certainly there is no more important milestone on the journey toward a world of law than the abolition of force as an instrument of national policy, beginning with the Kellogg-Briand Pact and culminating in the United Nations Charter. But an unforeseen and regrettable by-product of this new regime is the occasional temptation to smaller nations to behave with an irresponsibility that in earlier times would have been unthinkable. What has happened is that the use of force has been denounced by the great powers before a world organization has been perfected to the point where it can perform the function of enforcing international responsibility. While this interregnum lasts, the smaller and newer nations will naturally not be as deeply conscious of the need for legal protection of their rights as they once were.

On the other hand, it would be a mistake to overemphasize the impediments in the path of acceptance of international law by the newer countries. In the early stages of the Congo crisis there occurred an incident which was almost entirely overlooked in the general confusion. On September 11, 1960, the President of the Republic of the Congo addressed the following message to the United Nations:

I have the honor to request the United Nations:

\* \* \*

To assist the Congo to reactivate the courts. To this end I, with the Prime Minister, shall request the creation of a pool of jurists which could be drawn on, on the recommendation of the International Court, to fill vacant judicial posts.

(*Signed*) JOSEPH KASAVUBU
President of the Republic
of the Congo

Here is a demonstration of confidence in the International Court going even beyond acceptance of its compulsory jurisdiction. It is of unusual significance that the Congo, in its darkest hour of lawlessness, seeking for some established institution which could be trusted to provide the beginnings of a regime of law and justice, should turn to the International Court of Justice for help. It did this in spite of the fact that there was no one from the Negro countries of Africa on the Court. This episode serves as an eloquent reminder of the fact that the International Court can do much more than merely decide particular cases. It can stand as a bulwark of law in a world of turmoil and help maintain the atmosphere of law and the habit of law in international dealings.

Another evidence pointing toward the beginnings of

greater Asian and African trust in the International Court
is the fact that the last three cases filed with the Court
involve entirely Asian and African plaintiffs and defendants: *Cambodia* v. *Thailand, Liberia* v. *Union of South
Africa,* and *Ethiopia* v. *Union of South Africa.*

# (19)
# Law and Change

"THE LAW STANDS FOR THE STATUS QUO;
we want change."

This is the essence of an argument frequently made by
the representatives of the newly developing countries as
they press their struggle for rapid economic, political, and
cultural advancement. If real progress is to be made in
getting wholehearted acceptance by the newer nations of
a rule of law in international affairs, the most important
prerequisite is to get rid of, once and for all, the ground-
less notion that the law freezes the *status quo.* There are
a number of fallacies in this notion.

The first fallacy is the idea that change and progress
come about mostly as a result of changing laws. The
demonstrable historical fact is that the greatest change
and progress have always occurred when there was a
reasonably stable and reliable framework of law in existence. With the security and confidence provided by this
legal framework, the illimitable human and economic
drives of individuals and groups have been unleashed.

The result has been the transformation of the modern world.

One stable rule of law, the rule that agreements must be kept, has produced more rapid and far-reaching change in the world than all the governmental appropriations and expropriations in history.

As illustrations, we have only to compare the stagnation of the Middle Ages, accompanying a general breakdown in legal institutions and relationships, with the tremendous change and development that took place both during the period of the ascendancy of the legal system of Rome and during the period of modern commerce within the system of dependable legal relations worked out in modern times.

Another fallacy is the assumption that law itself is absolutely rigid and never adapts itself to the needs of the times. This is a mistake that is not apt to be made by a person versed in the history of the common law. Even under the codes of the civil law, however, the concept is more a matter of theory than of actual practice. As to international law itself, surely no one would assert that it has remained utterly unchanged since the time of Grotius. The three main sources of international law are custom, treaties, and the general principles of law recognized by civilized nations. Customs and practices obviously change over a period of time, although the change may be slow because it must conform to the practices of nations generally. Treaties are constantly being made and changed. As for the general principles of law, these too can presumably undergo some change as the principles accepted by the various major legal systems themselves slowly evolve and become perfected. At the same time judicial decisions, arbitral awards, and other elements of international law are constantly adding to the over-all body of substantive law.

Perhaps the best contemporary illustration of the way in which legal institutions can adapt themselves to the needs of changing times is the evolution of the United Nations and its component parts. Among the changes that have come about purely through custom and practice are the greatly increased role of the General Assembly, the emergence of the Secretary-General as a powerful operating executive agent, the growth of the international armed force and its use in such places as the Gaza strip and the Congo, and the adoption of such devices as the inquiry team dispatched to Laos to help keep order. All of these changes have come about without benefit of any formal change in law, in the sense of adoption of a Charter amendment or an amendment to the Statute of some component organization.

The final fallacy is the assumption that, on the international scene, there is no device for changing law comparable to legislation on the domestic scene. One is frequently told that, when a particular rule of law becomes intolerable domestically, it can always be changed by the act of the legislature, but that if a rule of law becomes intolerable at the international level, there is no comparable way in which to get it changed. This kind of argument would be easier to refute if a concrete example were brought forward of a rule of law that has perpetuated hardship on the international scene because of this alleged fatal deficiency.

The closest thing to legislation internationally is the adoption of multilateral treaties blanketing a particular area of law by agreement among a large number of nations. There are many such conventions in effect, and they are being made and altered constantly. A recent example is the revision of the law of the sea, which was initiated in two sessions at Geneva attended by practically every nation with an interest in the matter. These conferences adopted conventions modernizing the entire law of the sea with the exception of the width of the territorial waters, and this provision failed of agreement by only one vote. (These conventions are, of course, subject to ratification.) Another recent example is the adoption of a new regime for Antarctica by agreement of the nations affected. It may be objected that the changing of law by treaties is not really comparable to the changing of law by legislation, since under a treaty everybody affected has to agree to the particular change in the law. This is true. But it is also true that, in order to produce legislation, agreement must be reached not only between a majority of the representatives in the legislative body but sometimes with an independent executive. If less than this majority can be made to agree, nothing happens. At the international level, if less than a majority of the nations agree on a change, at least those who do agree can alter their legal relations more to their liking.

There are other ways in which international law may change. For example, the International Law Commission is constantly studying the clarification, revision, and modernization of international law. Its work was almost entirely adopted by the conferences on the law of the sea.

All kinds of international organizations, in and out of the United Nations structure, are engaged in making and revising rules having to some extent the effect of law.

All in all, while the concern about need for change in the law and absence of an international legislature may seem theoretically serious, it is difficult to find any evidence that this is a justifiable reason for mistrust of law by newly developing countries or by anyone else. The actual fact is that most of the changes that have taken place in international law and practice have been changes favorable to these very same newly developed countries. The most obvious and important illustration is the outlawing of force and aggression in international affairs.

# (20)
# World Law and Economic Development

THE ACCEPTABILITY OF INTERNATIONAL rule of law to the newly developing countries will be closely related to the extent to which they are convinced that it will further their plans for economic development.

We hear so much about vast expenditures for governmental economic and technical aid and about the tremendous upsurge in the newly developing countries that we may be misled into forming an erroneous notion of the true state of affairs. If the problem is viewed as one of progressively narrowing the gap between the richer and poorer countries, the fact is that we are losing ground in spite of all the efforts that have been made. The relative rate of economic development is greater in the established industrial nations than it is in the newly industrializing ones. The newer nations are acutely aware of this fact. One speaker after another from such countries as Ceylon, India, and Indonesia pointed out this disparity in the October meeting in 1957 of the GATT contracting parties.

At the end of 1959, of the $29.7 billion of American private foreign investment, 51 per cent went to Western Europe and Canada, 28 per cent to Latin America, 8 per cent to Asia and 3 per cent to Africa. Half of Asian and African investment was devoted to petroleum. From all the talk about Asia and Africa one might get the impression that these are the principal concern of our overseas investment activity. As these figures show, the amount of private capital going into Asia and Africa is relatively small.

The present theme is that the newly developing countries should accept world rule of law as their best hope of achieving their goals of economic development. Precisely what would "accepting world rule of law" consist of for this purpose, apart from subscribing generally to the jurisdiction of the International Court of Justice? The most important specific testing ground is the matter of legal agreements covering the protection of foreign investments. In a comparatively short span of years the world has witnessed expropriations of private investment on a vast scale in many parts of the world. The most grandiose examples are the confiscations attending the Communist revolutions in Russia and China and the consequent extension of the Communist system to other areas of Europe and Asia. But there have also been expropriations in such places as Iran, Egypt, Indonesia, Cuba, and elsewhere. In addition, there have been other less obvious interferences and harrassments. The net effect of all this has been to make the investors of private capital deeply conscious of the hazards of expropriation when confronted with the question whether to invest in a new country. Unfortunately this cause for hesitation coincides exactly with the moment at which the need for fresh capital on a vast scale in the newer countries has become acute. To make the situation even more poignant, it is common knowledge that capital is being generated in the United States at such a rate that it is becoming difficult for some major holders of capital, such as large insurance companies and trust funds, to find suitable outlets for their capital. One large insurance company is under the necessity of finding investments for $5,000,000 every day in the year. The problem, then, of matching capital supply and capital demand is becoming increasingly more pressing. One of the principal bottlenecks to the solution of this urgent problem is the absence of a reliable legal framework for investment in many, if not most, of the newer countries.

As a result, a number of specific efforts are underway to provide such a framework, either by adopting an agreed investment code or by formulating existing international law on the subject. The International Chamber of Commerce drew a code for fair treatment of foreign investments in 1949 and is still actively engaged in revising it and seeking ways to make it more acceptable. The Council of Europe has a project for an investment statute originating in the report of a study group in September, 1957. The German Society to Advance the Protection of Foreign Investments prepared an "International Convention for the Mutual Protection of Private Property Rights in Foreign Countries," which has been widely circulated by the society's president, Dr. Hermann Abs. Lord Hartley Shawcross and a group of English and continental international lawyers have prepared a "Convention on Foreign Investments" which has had extensive discussion. The International Bar Association attempted a formulation of principles of international law on this subject at Cologne in 1958, and a somewhat similar formulation was made by the International Law Association at its New York Conference in September, 1958. There may also be mentioned the proposal by the Prime Minister of Malaya at the fourteenth session of the United Nations Economic Commission for Asia and the Far East, a proposal of a multilateral convention by the European League for Economic Cooperation in February, 1958, and a resolution adopted by the Interparliamentary Union in Rio de Janeiro in July, 1958.

Most of these formulations are principally concerned with providing a workable rule for some kind of appropriate compensation in case of nationalization of private investment, the establishment of an impartial method of settling disputes under the agreement through reference to the International Court of Justice or some other tribunal, and the forbidding of discrimination between foreigners and nationals.

The greatest single flaw common to all of these proposals is quickly stated: They have not been adopted. A tremendous amount of thought, effort, and skill has gone into these drafts and formulations. But until recently, at any rate, the proposals have been largely drawn from the point of view of the investing countries, and the wishes and points of view of the recipient countries do not seem to have received adequate consideration.

There has been a notable exception to this one-sided approach, one which has not had sufficient attention. This was the proposal by the Prime Minister of Malaya made in a speech opening the meeting of the Economic Commission for Asia and the Far East in Malaya on March 5, 1958. The substance of his proposal has been accorded the support of a large number of newly developing countries in the United Nations. In his speech the prime minister first dealt with the need for governmental economic aid and governmental development plans. He then went on to say:

But I doubt whether international government aid, vital though it is, will ever be sufficient to meet all our needs. For this reason I suggest that more consideration be given to the promotion of the flow of private capital into Asian countries from more advanced countries in other parts of the world. I am aware that many countries represented here already attach importance to creating the right conditions to attract such private capital and that this subject has been discussed on many occasions sponsored by this Economic Commission. His Majesty's Government here in this country has certainly al-

ways made its stand clear on this subject, but I wonder
whether we should not all go further than these individual
statements and purely national measures.

I wonder whether it would not be a powerful incentive to
the attraction of private capital to Asia if those countries,
which decided as a matter of public policy that they wished
to attract such capital, were to come together through chan-
nels provided by the United Nations economic organisations
such as this, and were to draw up, in consultation with representatives of potential lender countries, an International
Charter by which they would agree to regulate their treatment of foreign private capital. I will not attempt to elaborate
this morning the details of such a Charter. As I see it, it would
have the object of assuring potential lenders that their just
rights and interests would be fully respected and protected;
it might also indicate to them the part they would be expected to play in promoting the development of both the human and natural resources in the receiving country; and last,
but by no means least, it would remove any fears that private
foreign investment might interfere with the sovereignty and
true national interests of the receiving country. Such a Charter would, of course, be a purely voluntary one open to signa-
ture by any country interested in promoting the international
flow of private capital. But I should hope that our neighbour-
ing countries in South East Asia in particular would be willing to take a lead in this matter. For as I have said before:
we and our neighbours in South East Asia have so many common problems that if we are to progress we must work together even more closely—perhaps even through the aegis
of some special committee or working party established by
this Commission.

But if, as I believe to be the case, we need more capital
both public and private I cannot help but think that if some

Charter such as that which I have suggested could be drawn up, it would constitute a powerful inducement to private enterprise in other countries of the world to lend to those less developed countries which they knew had publicly sub-scribed to it.

As one looks at the draft proposals that have been made, one cannot help wondering how they must appear from the point of view of the capital-receiving countries. These drafts take great pains to protect the interests of the investor against various kinds of expropriation and discrimination and to buttress these protective devices by provisions on enforcement which often have a faintly menacing tone. The provisions may all be perfectly rea-sonable, but to the newly developing countries it may seem that the rich and strong nations of the world are "ganging up" to protect their own self-interest and to impose their will upon the smaller nations.

Thus, in the New York *Times* of April 23, 1959, it is reported that the Pakistan delegate to the Interna-tional Chamber of Commerce, in the course of discussion of the Chamber's International Investment Code, "criti-cized private enterprise for laying too much emphasis on profit and too little on social responsibilities, such as sup-port for education and health projects."

It would be difficult for anyone at this point to enu-merate specific proposals for clauses in a draft convention addressed to the rights of the host country. These pro-posals must emanate from the host countries themselves. What is needed is a full-scale research project to find out exactly what the capital-receiving countries believe they should have in the way of protection and assurances in an international investment code. There have been some general clues, but much more work has to be done to find out specifically what they have in mind. Several broad themes keep recurring in their comments. One of them is that any such code must concern itself with the protection of the independence and sovereign rights of the recipient country. Another recurring theme has to do with the right of any nation to reserve control over its natural resources in the interests of its own people. Still another theme is the need for investors and investing countries to take a greater interest in the social, economic, and human needs of the people of the recipient country.

A thorough job of research on this topic, followed by the kind of conference proposed by the Malayan prime minister, might well produce a detailed and reliable set of proposals, the inclusion of which in an investment convention would multiply its chances of general acceptance.

There are those who say that, while this is all perfectly true, the purpose of an investment code is frankly to protect the investor and that therefore its one-sided character is justifiable. Whether this is so, as a matter of abstract logic, is not the question. The question is whether the host countries agree with this one-sided approach, for if they do not, any convention, however unassailable its intrinsic excellence, will remain a futile exercise in draftsmanship.

It may be that a leaf may be borrowed here, as in so many other international matters, from experience in labor negotiation and labor legislation. A skillfully drawn labor bill or contract will often go to great pains to balance out a provision on employer rights and duties with a corresponding provision on employee rights and duties, and vice versa. One may recall here the vigorous insistence by unions that the non-Communist affidavits for labor union leaders in the National Labor Relations Act be balanced by a requirement that all employers also take a non-Communist oath. The reason for this insistence was probably not that the unions seriously believed that communism among American business executives was a problem requiring legislative solution. Rather the reason was that, until the provision relating to union officers was balanced by one relating to corporate officers, the legislation contained a sort of implication which the labor movement regarded as insulting and discriminatory. This is not to imply that the provisions concerned with the interests of the host countries should be meaningless, face-saving makeweights inserted solely for their antiphonal effect. There will be many significant matters of substance in this category. At the same time the investing countries should realize that provisions which may seem either insignificant or superfluous to them may seem important to the host country. For example, the host country may want to include assertions of sovereign rights which are self-evident and undisputed in international law. If the recipient countries want such pronouncements included for reasons of their own, it would be the height of ineptitude for the investing countries to prejudice the acceptance of the convention by raising objections on the ground of alleged redundancy.

The general point of view here suggested is not altogether without precedent. In the Foreign Economic Assistance Act of 1950, for instance, there was the following passage in Title IV of the Act for International Development, in section 402(c): "In the case of investment this

involves confidence on the part of the people of the underdeveloped areas that investors will conserve as well
as develop local resources, will bear a fair share of local
taxes and observe local laws, and will provide adequate
wages and working conditions for local labor."

The efforts now being applied to the problem of the
protection of investment should take a new direction and
a new emphasis. One cannot help being impressed by the
amount of energy that is being devoted to this problem,
in the form of creation of associations, drafting and discussion of possible treaties, writing of books and articles,
conduct of special research projects, and holding of conferences. The suggestion here is that if a considerable
fraction of the resources and effort now devoted to this
issue could be focused on understanding and effectuating
the legitimate wishes of the recipient countries, we might
bring much nearer the day when we shall see a convention on international investments which is both workable and acceptable.

There is another promising approach to this problem
which is in much the same spirit. This is the devising of
various kinds of partnership agreements between the
host governments and the private foreign investors. Professor Wolfgang Friedmann of Columbia has an active
project in progress concerned with this approach and has
produced a number of publications showing its potentialities. The general idea is that, if the host government
itself has a large direct interest in the mutual investment,
this in itself tends to solve many of the most troublesome
problems, since obviously the government is not going to
adopt measures harrassing a venture in which it is itself
a partner.

Finally, it should be mentioned that there are numerous other measures that could be taken on the legal side in aid of international economic development. These include various revisions of tax laws both in the capital-receiving countries and in the capital-supplying countries, strengthening of the investment guarantee program under which the government of the investor provides a sort of insurance against various kinds of loss including confiscation, the clearing up of difficulties caused by the impact of anti-trust laws on foreign investment, the enormous job of unifying commercial laws and contracts in the interest of simplicity, the perfection and acceptance of arbitration and other dispute-settling mechanisms for foreign trade controversies, and the promising possibility, discussed in Chapter 2, of facilitating international investment by an all-out effort to collect and make readily available the laws bearing on investment of all the countries in the world.

# (21)

# Acceptance by Communist Countries

WE NOW COME TO THE INEVITABLE QUESTION: "But what about the Communists?"

Any concept of "world rule of law" would plainly be incomplete if it did not supply at least a hypothesis showing how the Communist countries might be brought within its orbit.

Let us look briefly at the difficulties and obstacles, which are relatively well-known, and then go on to try to make the most of such favorable factors as can be found. One fundamental obstacle is the Communist conception of the place of law and courts in the overall scheme of things. It would be rash to announce at any given moment what the Communist doctrine on this point is, since it has undergone four or five marked changes in the forty-year history of the Soviet Union. For present purposes it is sufficient to observe that, in Soviet theory, laws and courts have often been assigned a less independent status than in Western jurisprudence and have been treated more as components contributing to the overall purposes of the state. Similarly, as noted in the chapter on sovereignty under the law, it would be much more difficult to accommodate Soviet theory to the concept that sovereignty is within the law than any other legal tradition. Moreover, the classical Leninist idea of the inevitability of major clashes between communism and capitalism is difficult to reconcile with the premise that international disputes should be settled peaceably under law.

These are some of the basic difficulties, and there are many others. But since, in the past, practically all the emphasis has been on the difficulties and since very little attention has been given to the glimmers of hope for the beginnings of a solution, the effort here will be to concentrate on the latter. It should be understood in advance that this does not imply any unawareness of the severity and complexity of the problem nor any rosy prediction of the probabilities of a happy ending for the story. However long the odds may be, we have no choice. We must have a hypothesis on which to work which, if successful, would produce the desired result. Then at least we know where to put our efforts in the years ahead.

The first favorable factor that should be noted is the preoccupation of Soviet Communists with legality. It is a serious mistake to suppose that, because some of our concepts of law differ, the Communists are indifferent to legality as such. Such incidents as the secret trials and campaigns of terror under Stalin have left the impression in some minds of utter lawlessness and have tended to obscure the extent to which the concept of legality dominates much of Communist thought. The famous de-Stalinization speech of Khrushchev at the Twentieth Party Congress consisted mostly of a bill of particulars accusing Stalin of violations of socialist legality. The output of Soviet legal scholars is extensive and contains some of the most elaborate and detailed legal writing to be found anywhere. Several years ago lawyers returning from an international conference of lawyers in Warsaw reported that the speakers from Communist countries declared as strong a devotion to the rule of law as anyone—under a different name. They called it socialist legality and said that it must ultimately conform to the standards of what they called humanism. And what are these standards? Protection of the civil rights of individuals. Derivation of legal authority only from the consent of the people. Subjection of the state itself to law. Correction of actions of administrators by independent judges.

In short, whether they knew it or not, these Communist spokesmen were giving voice to the deepest traditions of Western law.

Some will say that this is only lip service. But even if this minimal estimate is used, it is important that the Communists believe it necessary to pay lip service to these ideas. It is something to build upon.

There are other favorable signs. Since the death of Stalin, there have been some significant liberalizations of Soviet laws and procedures bringing, for example, their protection of the rights of the accused in criminal cases somewhat closer to that afforded in Western jurisprudence. There is still a long way to go, but the direction of the movement is significant. Of course the direction could change, as it has often changed in the past, but at the moment our purpose is to assemble promising developments without stressing all the usual discounts applied to them.

The growth of a substantial and influential middle class in the Soviet Union and of the ownership of many of the familiar possessions of middle class life has ineluctably driven the Soviet Union to adopt many of the familiar rules that govern property relations in other countries. Here again it is easy for a person who carelessly equates Russian communism with Biblical or Brook Farm communism to leap to the conclusion that Russian Communists cannot possible understand legal ideas about property. In actual practice, with some exceptions, Soviet laws about private property are not much different from those of Western countries. People in the Soviet Union own such private property as houses, automobiles, summer homes, household appliances and furniture, and financial savings. As a matter of common sense their legal rules governing buying and selling, renting and leasing, stealing and embezzling, giving and inheriting turn out to be roughly the same as those of the common and civil law countries. The real differences appear when you come to income-producing instruments of production whose ownership, of course, is in the state. On the other hand, surprising as it may seem, it is perfectly possible to rent out real property in the Soviet Union. It is not uncommon for the owner of a house to divide it into apartments and make a tidy income by renting the apartments. Curiously, the renting of personal property, such as automobiles, is not permitted, although it is difficult to see why this distinction between real and personal property rentals persists.

There is no reason why one should be surprised by all this, since the Communist countries of Eastern Europe all have legal systems rooted in the past, with a strong inheritance of civil and Byzantine law. These traditions cannot be completely thrown off even by so drastic an event as a revolution. Moreover, the elementary rights and relationships growing out of property in a modern industrial society with a rising standard of living are apt to be rather similar and require similar protection in any country, whatever its political ideology.

Finally, so far as the Leninist idea of the inevitability of a colossal world struggle is concerned, the present Soviet leadership appears to be engaged in a genuine effort to superimpose a gloss on this text, leaving room for peaceful coexistence. The extended discussions between the Soviet and Chinese Communists late in 1960 seem to confirm this impression, while still leaving unresolved the basic disagreement between the Russians and the Chinese on this point. Similarly, the Leninist idea that treaties are "only made to be broken" is out of tune with the constantly repeated insistence in Soviet legal writing on the sanctity of treaties.

Combined with all this is the psychological fact that the Soviet Union and the Russian people are obviously anxious to convince the world that they are as good as anyone else in every department, and perhaps better. They go to great lengths to demonstrate that they are as powerful as anyone, as productive as anyone, as cultured as anyone. Why not also as law-abiding as anyone? Certainly it would be out of line with the Soviet Union's exertions in other fields to suppose that they would be willing, when it comes to the field of law, to assume the posture of outlaw in the world community.

These, then, are some of the elements on the credit side of the ledger. The next question is: By what practical means might they be translated into actual practices and institutions for settlement of disputes under law?

# (22)

# Acceptance of World Law Through Treaty Interpretation Clauses

IT WOULD BE UNREALISTIC TO ASSUME THAT, in the predictable future, the Soviet Union will file a declaration unreservedly accepting the compulsory jurisdiction of the International Court of Justice. The writer has taken part in a number of debates about the World Court and has listened to speaker after speaker announce that we cannot trust the International Court because there are two Communists on it. One has only to imagine similar debates going on in Moscow, with speaker after speaker announcing that the International Court cannot be trusted because there are thirteen non-Communists on it. It must be admitted that the latter is more understandable than the former—although a thorough understanding of the Court's record for judicial integrity ought to be a complete answer in both instances. When the present composition of the Court is coupled with the Soviet attitude toward the place of law and courts in relation to the state, it seems reasonably clear that full acceptance of the Court's jurisdiction by the Soviet Union in the near future is not sufficiently probable to justify making that approach the main line of our efforts.

In the last analysis the most dependable motivation in human affairs, whether national or individual, is self-interest. This is why, in discussing the prospects of greater acceptance of world law by the newly developing countries, stress was placed on the strong interest these countries have in accepting a framework of law which would stimulate and facilitate economic development. Is there some comparable special self-interest motive that might propel the Soviet Union in the direction of settlement of disputes under law? The attempt here will be to show, by at least one example, that there is and that it centers round the relation between successful disarmament and increased standard of living in the Soviet Union.

For a number of years there have been two main themes in Soviet policy. One theme is domestic: The Soviet Union is determined to overtake and surpass the United States in production and consumer standard of living. The other theme is international: The Soviet Union calls for "general and complete disarmament." There is a direct relation between the two themes. The reason is this: The Soviet Union is now devoting almost twice as large a proportion of its gross national product to arms and arms-supporting industry as the United States. Its total gross national product is not much more than half that of the United States. How can the Soviet Union deliver on its promises of a greatly improved consumer standard of living and still burn up this proportion of its national energy and resources in the armaments race?

The dominant self-interest force, then, in Soviet policy would seem to be its interest in achieving a workable disarmament program so as to be able to make good on

some of its promises for improved living standards. Assume then, at least for the sake of argument, that a workable disarmament agreement would genuinely be in the
Soviet interest.

This leads directly to the next question: What does it
take to make the disarmament agreement workable? Of
course, there are many essentials, but there is one which
is directly relevant to the present problem. Experience
has demonstrated that any treaty, to be successful, should
have built into it a reliable and impartial mechanism for
interpretation and settlement of disputes under the treaty.
Clauses in international treaties providing for such interpretation and dispute-settlement are known as compromissory clauses. They occur in hundreds of treaties.
For example, they are practically standard language in
all treaties of friendship, commerce, and navigation made
by the United States. The last sixteen such treaties contain a compromissory clause. The clause may entrust interpretation and dispute-settling either to the International Court of Justice or to some other tribunal.

It does not take much imagination to forecast what
would happen in a disarmament treaty if it did not contain some such mechanism for settling disputes of interpretation. We have had a number of treaties with the
Soviet Union, and, in the absence of a compromissory
clause, the number of claims of treaty-breaking by the
Soviet Union is so great that the United States State Department has compiled an entire book of them. For its
part the Soviet Union makes similar charges against the
United States and does not, for one moment, admit that
it has ever broken any of these treaties. The Soviet Un-

ion has, by its account, merely interpreted them differently or applied to them certain doctrines or theories on termination of the binding force of treaties. Indeed, it is probably true that most of our present disputes and tensions with relation to the Soviet Union have their roots in some treaty and in recriminations about bad faith in complying with the treaty.

Against this backdrop of experience it would be foolhardy in the extreme to take the most complex and crucial problem of our time—disarmament—and plunge it into the same kind of treaty arrangement which has produced so much strife in the past. The ink would hardly be dry on the signatures before disputes of interpretation would begin to flare up. Necessarily a disarmament treaty will be crammed with detailed provisions, expressed in terms having flexible meanings. Picture a Russian inspection team pointing to a factory filled with rugged-looking vehicles and asserting: "Those are tanks." The Americans insist they are not tanks but trucks. The Russian inspection team reports to its government that the Americans are already cheating on their agreement. The Russians then announce that they will reciprocate. Another Russian inspection team sees a large number of figures in uniform in Yankee Stadium and says, "What are all those soldiers doing there?" The Americans say, "Those are not soldiers. Those are Boy Scouts having a Jamboree." The Russians reply that they have never heard of a Jamboree but they know uniforms when they see them and once more the report goes back that American youth is being put into uniform in violation of the agreement. Meanwhile, our inspectors see a large encampment of young people and are told that these are merely a civilian youth corps. The Americans reply cynically that they have heard of civilian youth corps before and report back to Washington that the Russians are training soldiers in the guise of a youth corps. And so it goes. Each report of a violation invites a reciprocal pull-back. In the absence of an impartial way of settling the disputes, the recriminations grow and the pull-backs increase until, instead of a working disarmament arrangement, the result is greater bitterness and hostility than would have existed even if no treaty had been written in the first place.

Of course, the illustrations above are somewhat fanciful, but they are designed to bring out the serious point that there are all kinds of "para-military" goods and personnel and factories that would unavoidably give rise to controversies of interpretation on a major scale. The treaties that have been discussed contain all kinds of phasings which must take place in proper sequence and coordination, all kinds of inspection rights and limitations about which people in both countries would be extremely sensitive, and all kinds of definitions and distinctions which would require constant interpretation.

Now how are these questions of interpretation going to be settled? The only workable way to do it is to have a judicial type of body. The interpreting of treaties is intrinsically a legal and judicial function. It will not work to entrust this kind of decision to an administrative office or a commission. Suppose there is a mixed commission with three Americans and three Russians entrusted with this task. It is perfectly obvious what would happen. The commission would split on national lines and there would be a deadlock on every decision. Administrative officers and commissioners have neither the competence, the tradition, the body of law and principle, nor the temperament to make the kind of impartial decisions that would be necessary. By contrast, a judicial or at least quasi-judicial tribunal would approach these questions, not only with the full integrity of traditional judicial impartiality behind them, but also with the entire body of international law governing the detailed questions of how to interpret contracts, agreements, and treaties. This impartial tribunal could be the International Court of Justice itself or, if this is not acceptable to the Russians, perhaps a special panel of the Court. Failing this, it could be a special tribunal manned by judges of assured impartiality.

Whatever the detailed structure of the tribunal might be, the important point is this: If the necessity for making a disarmament treaty workable drives the parties to the establishment of an impartial tribunal for the settlement of their disputes under law, then we have achieved the first major breakthrough toward a system of law capable of accommodating both Communist and non-Communist countries.

If this arrangement worked out satisfactorily in a disarmament agreement, it would be a short step to inclusion of such a clause in other treaties with the Soviet Union. Eventually agreement might be reached even to insert such a clause in some troublesome past treaties. In view of the dominant role assigned by Communist theory to treaties in international law, it can be seen that over a period of time this process would gradually blanket a considerable area of legal relations with the Soviet Union into an orderly regime of law.

One cannot leave this subject without also asking, "What about Communist China?" At this stage of Communist China's development and of our relations with that country, one can only say that the difficulties in the case of Communist China are probably the same as with the USSR but of much greater magnitude. Communist China seems to be traveling something like the same path traveled by the Soviet Union at a distance of several decades. The hopeful signs that have begun to appear in the Soviet Union are hardly visible in Communist China. One can only hope that the same evolution, the same pressures, and the same measures that we have observed and must work on in relation to the Soviet Union may perhaps someday be effective with Communist China. There is one present advantageous factor concerning Communist China which did not exist twenty-five years ago in relation to the Soviet Union; the USSR itself may act as a steadying influence. For this reason any progress that can be made toward bringing the Soviet Union within the framework of world law may prove to be progress also toward a similar, though more distant, outcome in the case of Communist China.

# PART FOUR

# Compliance with World Law

🀲🀲🀲🀲🀲🀲🀲🀲🀲🀲🀲🀲🀲🀲🀲🀲🀲🀲🀲🀲🀲🀲

## (23)
## Is International Law Obeyed?

THE FOURTH COMPONENT IN AN INTERNA-
tional legal system is compliance.

It is a curious fact that, although many people seem to
worry more about how world law is to be enforced than
about any other item, in practice this question may prove
to be the least worrisome of all. The historical fact is
that there have been very few cases of noncompliance
with the decisions of international tribunals. Among the
hundreds of awards that have been made, authorities
have been able to find only a few cases in which the
question of refusal to comply was present. The largest
figure that the writer has seen of the number of such instances is twenty.

In the history of the Permanent Court of International
Justice, there is not a single instance of failure to com-

ply. As for the International Court of Justice, there was noncompliance with one portion of the judgment of one case. This was the failure of Albania to comply with so much of the order in the Corfu Channel case as required payment of damages. Even this is a somewhat shaky illustration, in view of the fact that Albania maintained throughout the case that, while it had submitted to the Court's jurisdiction for other purposes, it had not so submitted for the purpose of assessment of damages.

This remarkable record cannot be explained away by the assertion, sometimes heard, that the cases involved were not very important anyway. Of course, some of the cases involved relatively minor matters. On the other hand, there are plenty of cases involving major national interests and major commitments of national prestige. The suit between Norway and Denmark on ownership of East Greenland, a territory of great size and of emotional and historical importance, can hardly be waved aside as trivial. Indeed, regardless of the amount of land involved, any boundary dispute by nature is apt to involve a deep commitment of national pride and sentiment, and boundary disputes are one of the most common categories of both arbitral and judicial settlement.

As a matter of pure economic interest, the books are full of multimillion dollar awards that have been paid, such as the $5.5 million award against the United States made by the Halifax Commission in the Fisheries Concession case in 1871, the $15.5 million award against Britain in the "Alabama" arbitration, for the depradations of the vessel "Alabama" during the Civil War, and the $12.2 million award against the United States and in favor of Norway in 1923 for ships requisitioned in World War I. In all these cases there was strong national feeling aroused in the losing countries, but the awards were invariably paid.

The real explanation of this record of compliance seems to be this: Once matters have been brought to the point where the parties accept both the substantive body of law under which disputes are to be decided and the machinery of law, they are by then "in so deep" that it becomes unthinkable to refuse compliance when the decision has been rendered. If this is so, it is of first-rate importance in the assessment of priorities among our efforts. It seems to teach that our first concern should be to improve the body of law and the machinery of law to the point where they become acceptable to the nations that must use the system. We should not, in other words, conceive of the task of achieving international rule of law as a matter first of creating a powerful international police force to guarantee enforcement. In any event the police force cannot undertake enforcement action until some authoritative tribunal has decided who is right and who is wrong in the particular controversy on the basis of an established body of law. As has just been indicated, once this decision has been made by an acceptable tribunal under an acceptable body of law, the chances are that the police will not have to be called in, any more than they are on the domestic scene, to ensure compliance.

If the record of compliance with international awards is at least as good as that of compliance with domestic decisions, and perhaps better, why is it that some critics

go about ridiculing international law and saying that it
is something no one pays any attention to? The answer
probably lies in the failure to distinguish between decisions of tribunals and unilateral assertions of legal rights.
We allege that Country X has repeatedly broken treaties. We conclude and assert that Country X has no respect for international law. But does Country X admit
this? Certainly not; it will give a formula to show that
it did not really break a treaty but interpreted it or applied some doctrine of modification or discharge. We may
be positive we are right. But as long as matters are in
this posture, it is impossible to say with impartiality and
finality that Country X has broken international law. But
let the case be taken to an impartial tribunal, where the
law is applied to the facts and where a decision of unassailable authenticity is rendered. Then, when the rights
and the wrongs are settled beyond question, we shall have
a reliable test of the degree of compliance with law. It is
the record of compliance judged on this basis that gives
hope that we can profitably push ahead with the strengthening of the structure of law without waiting for the
day to come, if it ever comes, when some kind of global
political authority comparable to national governments
will stand behind the decisions of international tribunals, armed with overwhelming physical force.

# (24)
# Why Is Law Obeyed?

MUCH OF THE DISCUSSION OF THE POTEN-
tialities of world rule of law is carried on under the un-
proved assumption that the only motivation for obedience
to law is fear of the exercise of force by some political
superior. If this assumption is correct, it would have a
profound bearing on the direction that profitable exertions in this area ought to take. If the assumption is un-
founded, we ought to know that too. Certainly this is an
issue which should not be left to speculation and rhetoric.

Why do people obey the law? One way to get the answer to this question is for each person to ask himself:
Why do I obey the law? Some of the motivations that act
on individuals may not be directly relevant to states, but
many of them are relevant.

Of course, the fear of the policeman's club is one such
motive. The degree to which this motive assumes importance for a particular individual will probably be affected
by the nature of his relation to his society. The hard-
ened criminal knows no other motive, and even this motive is not enough to deter him from law-breaking. The
normal responsible citizen, by contrast, seldom or never
gives a thought to the possibility that he might be made
the subject of physical enforcement of the laws, yet he
obeys thousands of laws and regulations every day. Why
does he do it? There are many reasons.

The habit of law is one. Suppose you are driving alone

on a dark night in a remote part of the country. Out in the middle of nowhere you come to a crossroads at which there is a large red sign saying "STOP." You may be positive that there is no one for miles around. Yet you stop. The chance of detection and punishment is virtually zero. No question of ethics or public opinion is involved. You simply stop because the habit of obeying the law makes you stop.

The same motivation undoubtedly operates at the international level. A large part of international relations runs smoothly because of observance of rules of diplomatic usage established over centuries. No superstate enforces these rules, but it would seldom occur to any state to break them.

A second important motive would be principle. Much, but by no means all, of law has a moral or ethical content and is the effort of a society to translate its moral standards into formal rules. Here again, the normal responsible citizen does not commit rape or burglary whenever the opportunity presents itself with zero chance of detection and punishment. It is a rare individual who will help himself to a paper or to a box full of nickels from an unattended newsstand. For many people this rule of conduct also has a religious base. Of the various motivations here listed, this one has probably the least carryover to the actions of nation-states. Nevertheless, states act through individuals who must necessarily be affected both by their own personal moral codes and by the cumulative force of the moral standards of the people they represent.

Public opinion is undoubtedly one of the strongest motivations, both for individuals and for nations. No one wants to be branded an outlaw. Our typical responsible citizen would much rather pay a hundred dollar fine than have his name appear in the paper as having been convicted of driving while intoxicated. On the international scene the force of world opinion is formidable and appears to be gaining strength. It was world opinion, and not world government or physical force, that turned back the British and French invasion of Suez. World opinion spoke, not only through the protests of individual governments, but through the reaction of the General Assembly of the United Nations. The General Assembly had no power to send a force against the British and French. It could only send a resolution against them. But a resolution did the job.

Somewhat related is the apprehension of group ostracism. An individual law-breaker faces the risk of being expelled from his club and otherwise cut off from his community. The international law-breaker may run the risk of being expelled from the United Nations. To most nations of the world, particularly the smaller and newer nations, this would be an unspeakable calamity. To most of the smaller countries status as member of the United Nations is the one fact that makes nationhood meaningful and significant in modern times. It gives the head of state or the United Nations representatives the right to travel to New York, hobnob with counterparts from all the big countries, lunch with foreign secretaries and even presidents, and, above all, to express their country's view and cast their country's vote on terms of equality with any other country.

Still another motive for compliance with law is economic pressure. Why does not the merchant cheat you whenever possible in subtle ways that the police cannot prevent? He does it because of the economic fact that he would be boycotted and his business would suffer if he indulged in law-breaking. Similarly, on the international scale there are many ways in which economic pressures can operate against an international law-breaker.

There are a number of other motives that could be cited, but the most important of all has been left until the last. This motive is, once more, our unworthy but reliable motive of self-interest. This self-interest can express itself in both negative and positive form. The negative form is fear—fear of retaliation and fear of the reciprocal lawlessness that the initial lawlessness may breed. Concern about possible arrest for battery has sometimes deterred a right cross to the chin, but ten times as often the first blow has been deterred by the apprehension of a return blow. So on the international level the knowledge that lawbreaking invites lawbreaking is a major deterrent to everything from breaches of the niceties of diplomatic protocol to outright aggressions.

There is also a positive way of stating the self-interest motive. Most people obey the laws because they prefer to give up a certain amount of individual license for the gain of living in an orderly, peaceful society. This motive looms proportionately even larger when applied to observance of international law.

Why does a nation accept a judicial or arbitral award handing over part of its sacred national territory to another country? The principal answer is probably that the loser would rather give up some territory and gain a world in which disputes are settled under law and not by violence. In his speech to the University of Delhi in 1959 President Eisenhower summed up this thought:

We will all have to remind ourselves that under this system of law one will sometimes lose as well as win. If an international controversy leads to armed conflict, everyone loses; if armed conflict is avoided, everyone wins. It is better to lose a point now and then in an international tribunal and gain a world in which everyone lives in peace under a rule of law.

# (25)
# Strengthening Nonforce Compliance

IT IS A MISTAKE TO ASSUME THAT PHYSIcal force is the only item in the international armory of sanctions for compliance with law. There are many other sanctions, some of them in particular cases even more effective than force. These include diplomatic sanctions, economic measures, attachment of property belonging to the debtor's estate, enforcement through municipal courts, various kinds of enforcement through international organizations, and enforcement measures under international arrangements apart from the United Nations. The availability of such measures should be constantly kept in mind as a reminder that strengthening of the enforcement of world law should proceed, not just through the strengthening of international police forces and the like, but equally through the strengthening of every other kind of nonforce sanction that can be devised.

A good example of a nonforce compliance device of obvious potency is that of the International Civil Aviation Organization. If its council finds that a member nation has refused to comply with a final decision of the International Court of Justice or an arbitral body, the contracting states undertake not to allow the airline of the offending state to operate in their territory. A more crushing sanction could hardly be imagined. Indeed, so far as international aviation activities are concerned, this action is a death sentence for the commerce of the recalcitrant state.

Adaptations of this type of device and counterparts tailored to other forms of international regulation can undoubtedly be worked out as needed by agreement.

Economic pressures may be undertaken both individually and collectively. An example of individual economic pressure appears to be the Lena Goldfields case in which the United Kingdom, by tying its negotiations for a trade agreement to the arbitral award against the USSR, successfully induced the USSR to comply with the award. Collective economic measures might be undertaken through withholding of credits by such organizations as the World Bank, by collective economic boycotts of an offending nation, and in many other ways.

Diplomatic pressures are a traditional form of enforcement. A recent example is the action of the Organization of American States against Trujillo and against Castro.

Sometimes more direct methods are available in particular cases, such as the seizure of property belonging to the debtor state, either within the creditor country or sometimes within third countries, and the enforcement of international judgments through the courts and enforcement machinery of particular countries. The obvious way to strengthen these forms of enforcement is to maximize the situations under local law in which the machinery of municipal law can be pressed into service for these purposes. Oscar Schachter has suggested the following legal propositions applicable to the seizure of property in a third country as an enforcement measure:

*1.* That states are entitled under international law (and possibly may be considered under a duty) to assist in the execution of a decision of the International Court, if that decision has not been complied with and the successful party requests such assistance;

*2.* That such assistance may include transferring to the judgment creditor assets of the judgment debtor which are located in the territory of the third state without obtaining the consent of the debtor estate and without obtaining the sanction of the Security Council or a further decision of the International Court;

*3.* That the right of the third state to effect such transfer is subject to a duty on its part to take necessary measures to safeguard any competing claims of other parties as, for example, by providing for judicial control as to the respective claims of all parties.

Schachter, who is head of the General Legal Division of the United Nations, states that these propositions are implicit in the action taken by the United States,

France, and the United Kingdom leading to the Monetary Gold case and that it is fair to say that the principles were regarded by the three governments as consistent with the requirements of international law. He also concludes that there is no insuperable obstacle to the enforcement of international judgments generally by municipal courts as a result of the possible jurisdictional immunity of the respondent state as a sovereign nation. One reason is that the obligation under the United Nations Charter to carry out the judgments of the International Court should prevail over a claim of immunity. Another has to do with the distinction, which is more highly developed in some European countries than in the United States, between commercial activity by a state and governmental activity, with immunity in domestic courts attaching only to the latter.

The United Nations Charter has an express provision on enforcement of International Court decisions in Article 94(2): "If any party to a case fails to perform the obligations incumbent upon it under a judgment rendered by the Court, the other party may have recourse to the Security Council, which may, if it deems necessary, make recommendations or decide upon measures to be taken to give effect to the judgment." There appears to be no limit or restriction on the kind of measures or recommendations that could be adopted under this section. Among the measures specifically mentioned in Article 41 are "complete or partial interruption of economic relations and of rail, sea, air, postal, telegraphic, radio, and other means of communication, and the severance of diplomatic relations."

Finally, since one of the strongest forces for compliance with international law has always been world opinion, it follows that the progressive building up of stronger world opinion insisting on respect for international law is one of the most promising avenues of strengthening compliance. As observed in the case of the Suez invasion, the vehicle for expressing this opinion may be the General Assembly, which has power under Article 10 to take up questions of noncompliance with the Court's judgments and to recommend action to member states.

Hence, there are many and varied nonviolent weapons at the disposal of the international community which, if strengthened and used to the full, could go a long way toward taking care of the problem of compliance.

# (26)
# The Place of Force in World Law

UP TO THIS POINT THE EFFORT HAS BEEN to make the most of the possibilities inherent in non-force compliance measures. The reason is a practical one. At this stage in history, with ultimate control of force lodged in national rather than international hands, we must do the best we can with what we have. There is always danger, when this kind of approach is adopted, of being laid open to the suspicion of undue optimism and of failure to recognize the realities of today's cold war world. It is perfectly true that, if one of the major military powers of the world were absolutely determined to defy an international judgment, it would probably not be deterred from the attempt by the nonforce sanctions described. It is also true, as one is sometimes reminded by the skeptical, that if massive land armies were to start grinding their way from the Soviet Union across Europe, there would be little that the International Court or international law or nonviolent sanctions could do to meet that emergency. But this assumes a relentless determination to defy law and world opinion, to break the peace, whatever the cost and risk of retaliation.

While this sort of hypothesis is often put forward in the name of "realism," the question remains whether it is a realistic assumption that this kind of determination and this kind of action is the primary danger to peace in today's world. We should never forget that, in the episode most closely resembling this hypothesis—the invasion of Suez—two of the most powerful nations in the world, Britain and France, were turned back from a military invasion without use of an international military force. It is probably closer to "realism" to note that threats to peace nowadays take the form, not of overt physical aggressions by obvious military invasions, but of a number of identifiable international disputes, such as Berlin, Suez, boundary disputes, aerial incidents, expropriations, and the like, which if not settled might progressively lead to hostilities.

These preliminary observations about the place of force in world law are intended to put the subject in proper perspective and to correct the superficial assumption that nonforce and limited force measures are, after all, not very significant because they could not cope with a powerful international gangster if it should decide to run amuck with all guns blazing.

Throughout this book the effort has been to find ways of building a world legal system without relying on United Nations Charter revision or other major change in the world's constitutional framework. It is, therefore, appropriate that the same approach be attempted for the problem of strengthening an international force to support international law.

Backing world law with force is inextricably intertwined with the matter of disarmament. The strength and usefulness of an international force cannot be judged in absolute terms, no matter what its size. It must be judged in relation to the national forces still in being at any given time. The process of disarmament, in turn, is intertwined with and dependent on the development of international rule of law. A relatively disarmed world with a powerful international force is simply not going to come into existence except as a satisfactory dispute-settling system is simultaneously developed. Armaments have not been built up entirely out of sheer "cussedness." They have been built up, in part at least, to perform a legitimate function: that of trying to protect the state against wrongful infringements of its rights, including its right to security.

It is this recognition of the interrelationship between law, disarmament, and the international security force that led to the American disarmament proposal in June,

1960, which was described by Secretary of State Christian Herter at the National Press Club as follows:

To assure a world of peaceful change, we should project a second stage of general disarmament. Our objective in this second stage should be twofold:

First, to create certain universally accepted rules of law which, if followed, would prevent all nations from attacking other nations. Such rules of law should be backed by a world court and by effective means of enforcement—that is, by an international armed force.

Second, to reduce national armed forces, under safeguarded and verified arrangements, to the point where no single nation or group of nations could effectively oppose this enforcement of international law by international machinery.

We are more apt to make genuine progress in relation to an effective international force if we keep before us a mental picture of a phased process in which gradual disarmament takes place, while simultaneously the process of strengthening both the international armed force and the international body and machinery of law go forward.

It is typical of the United Nations structure, just as it has been typical of the structure of the United States government, that far-reaching expansions of activity and changes in roles of component parts can take place without constitutional or Charter amendment. There is nothing in the United States Constitution creating the system of cabinet departments, or the vast bureaucracy of regulatory and administrative agencies, or the two-party political system, or the sweeping rearrangement of power between the federal and state governments and between the executive, judicial, and legislative branches. Similarly, without United Nations Charter revision, we have witnessed the great enlargement of the powers of the Secretary-General, the markedly enhanced role of the General Assembly which is theoretically limited to "recommendations," and the growth of an international security force.

There is no reason to doubt, therefore, that the evolution of an international force under law sufficient to keep the peace could at least theoretically be accomplished without a basic change in the constitutional structure of the United Nations. Let us look briefly at the background of the international force and its development to the present time and then attempt to construct a rough picture of what such a force might ultimately look like if the development proceeded to its logical conclusion.

The idea of an international military force is not entirely new. As long ago as 1910 the United States Congress suggested creating a commission which would study "constituting the combined navies of the world [into] an international force for the preservation of universal peace" in connection with arms limitations. In 1919 a joint military force under an international general staff was proposed by the French government, and the suggestion was renewed in more detailed form by the same government in 1932, in both instances in connection with disarmament proposals. At the Dumbarton Oaks Conference in 1944 both the Soviet Union and the Chinese delegation called for an international air force. The result was a provision in Article 45 of the Charter which obliges member states to "hold immediately available national air force contingents for combined international enforcement action." Article 43 of the Charter provides generally that all members of the United Nations shall make available to the Security Council, on its call and in accordance with a special agreement or agreements, armed forces and other assistance and facilities necessary to maintain international peace and security. However this obligation is to arise only upon the conclusion of special agreements, and these agreements have never been made. As a result, the United Nations forces assembled for action in Korea in 1950 and in the Middle East in 1956 were not the result of a regular advance creation of available contingents. The Korean force became largely the responsibility of the United States to assemble from among the nations willing to contribute. The Middle East force was mainly made up of contingents furnished by nations with relatively small military forces. The same was true of the Congo force.

The evolution of the international force, even with the Korean, Middle East, and Congo precedents, is at a very early stage. The exact legal authority for particular types of action, the limitations on the United Nations force once it goes into action, the purposes for which it may or may not be used, and the measures it may or may not employ are all matters on which law is being evolved by practice and precedents. One thing is clear: as a result of the inexorable demands of events, the world is gradually becoming accustomed to the idea of an actual fighting international force. Of course, the Korean action involved a great deal of fighting, but from the point of view of building up a true international force the significance of the action was diminished by the fact that in form it appeared to consist rather of the United Nations calling on members to supply an armed force, as distinguished from the creation of a regular United Nations force as such. The United Nations force in the Gaza strip is more truly an international force, but this unit has exerted its influence principally by symbolic presence rather than by actual fighting. With the advent of the Congo episode there was witnessed the formation of a real international force, organized by and answerable to the Secretary-General under Security Council authority. This force, though "noncombative" in theory, has found it necessary in self-defense to become engaged in active fighting, with resultant casualties on both sides. The force in the Congo is not an example of the sending of a force by the United Nations against an unwilling and recalcitrant law-breaker. The United Nations force is present by invitation. Nevertheless, its function is that of preserving law and order and preventing the kind of anarchy that might lead to a breach of the peace. The actual unfolding of the Congo story is a good illustration of how practice born of necessity can apparently expand the boundaries of limited authority to the point where the entire nature of the operation seems to be transformed. Thus, the United Nations force in the Congo was supposed to shoot only in self-defense. The expectation may have been that, as in the Gaza strip, the force would stand mainly as a show of United Nations presence, which would keep order without the necessity of resorting to bloodshed. As matters have turned out, the necessity for self-defense has arisen so often that, while the theory of firing only in self-defense is presumably maintained, the United Nations force inevitably looks more and more like a regular fighting contingent. However, having begun its operation by invitation, the force found itself being ordered to get out by Lumumba, which it did not do, and to submit to all sorts of restrictive orders by Mobutu, which it also resisted. It seems clear that, although invitation may have been necessary to set this kind of United Nations intervention in motion in the first place, this does not imply that the force acts only by permission from that point on, either as to the duration of its stay or as to the details of its activities. This seems to make good sense, since any other rule would make it impossible for the United Nations force to accomplish its mission of helping the country bring order out of anarchy.

These developments are cited merely to suggest that, when we appraise the potentialities of future evolution of the United Nations force within the present constitutional framework, we should not underestimate the flexibility with which institutions sometimes adapt themselves to the demands made on them, especially when the pressure of necessity is severe.

As various kinds of United Nations forces continue to evolve in response to various crises, it may be useful to identify, in addition to the kind of gradual steps that are contributing to this evolution, the ultimate form of a force that might result from this process, together with some of the details about its composition and administration. Of course, any such exercise must necessarily be viewed as merely illustrative of what could conceivably be done, since details of this kind will in fact depend on a host of variables which cannot now be predicted. As to size of such a force, since it must ultimately be stronger than any combination of national armaments that might be pitted against it, the strength of the force cannot be stated in absolute terms but would be dependent on the relative size of national armaments at any given point. Theoretically, an absolute limit beneath which national armaments cannot be expected to fall might be stated, since a certain minimum would always be considered appropriate for the maintenance of internal order. It has been estimated that, on the assumption of a reasonably successful disarmament process, the size of the international force might ultimately be around 500,000. Because of the potential idealistic appeal of this kind of force, coupled with the provision of good salaries and incidental benefits, it should be possible to staff such a force with young people of high quality without the necessity for any kind of international selective service. The distribution by nationalities should be such that no single nation would have more than a very small percentage of the force represented. Moreover, in the light of the experience in the Congo, it now seems desirable that the nationalities should not be clustered into separate units but should be commingled throughout the force, if this is practicable. Similarly, the command structure should be subject to regular rotation among nationalities. The force should be stationed at its own bases at strategic points around the world. It should be liberally equipped with air transport facilities, paratroop equipment, and other aids to mobility, because of the unusual importance of its ability to reach trouble spots promptly. The planning for the size and composition of an international force must constantly look in two directions. It must aspire to sufficient size and effectiveness to do the job assigned to it. On the other hand, it should be so adjusted, both as to size and as to detailed constitution, that it would not give rise to fears of a Frankenstein monster that will take over the world. Although superficially the postulated mathematical preponderance of strength in the central force might seem to lend some support to such fears, a closer look at the realities of such a situation will serve to dispel them. The force would be made up of people drawn from dozens of nationalities, all of whom expect to serve for a limited time and then resume their normal lives and friendships in their home countries. Such people would have small appetite for becoming the hated tools of some power-mad potential world dictator. Moreover, the force would be widely scattered geographically and would have a rotating command; thus, having no single industrial base to support it, it would be incapable of any sustained autonomous activity.

A force of this size and character could presumably be built gradually without a revision of the United Nations Charter, if the maximum use were made of Charter provisions and precedents already available. The immediate administrative control over the force, in the absence of any other available official, would presumably remain with the Secretary-General, since he is the only person in a position to take everyday executive action.

A question of crucial importance is: By what process, or by whose decision, is the force set in motion? Since there are several types of situation that might call for action, there might be several answers to this question.

The first situation would be a simple overt invasion of a country's territory. If such an invasion were witnessed by the persons in administrative control of the international force at some point in the world, there would be neither time nor occasion for anything other than a direct administrative decision by the force's controlling body to order the invaders to halt and retire and to back the order by immediately moving international units to the scene. Similarly, if an imminent offensive aerial or missile attack were detected, for example by international inspectors under a disarmament agreement, the right of an international force to take direct action would be clear. Ample analogy can be found in domestic law for the distinction between this kind of peremptory administrative action in emergencies and the normal procedures of law enforcement. Thus, a police officer who sees a burglar climbing through the window of a church can on his own authority make the decision to arrest him on the spot and may use such force as is necessary. By contrast, recall the case of the two ministers who both claimed the legal right to the pulpit of a church in Brooklyn. If the policeman on the beat had been called in, could he have made a legal decision between the two and then have arrested and detained the loser? Certainly not. The normal domestic law enforcement procedure always involves the judicial function and the issuance of warrants, informations, indictments and, of course, convictions and sentences.

Since the function of the police includes not only defending right against wrong but also preventing breaches of the peace as such, an international force should also have the power, wherever violence has occurred or is imminent, to step into contested territories and prevent further clashes. Just as such a force might have been able to act to stop the invasion of South Korea by North Korea, so also it might even occupy disputed areas between China and India for the sole purpose of preventing violence—recognizing that the ultimate question of legal rights in particular territories must later be settled by other means. It would be highly desirable to work out more detailed understandings on the conditions under which virtually automatic action by an international force could take place. As noted above, Secretary Herter has stressed "the need to create certain universally accepted rules of law which, if followed, would prevent all nations from attacking other nations."

In addition, there would of course be the use of the international force in situations such as the Congo problem, where the essence of the problem seems to be the existence of a degree of lawlessness which, if uncorrected, might spread and precipitate a breach of the peace. The Security Council has broad powers under Chapter VII of the Charter to take measures involving the use of force when necessary to maintain or restore international peace and security.

Finally, there are the cases in which the International Court of Justice has made an authoritative decision and in which the enforcement of that decision appears to require the use of force. Here again, although there has been some difference of opinion expressed on this point, it seems clear that the Security Council could use an international force directly to support a binding decision of the International Court of Justice.

These, then, are some of the ways in which world law is now being backed by force and can more effectively be backed by force in the future, through the evolution of present embryonic organisms into ultimate full-grown institutions capable of keeping world order. But it cannot be stressed too often that the heart of the matter is not force; it is law. Too often it is assumed that, if we could only create a decisively powerful international police force under central control, the problem of achieving world order would be largely solved. This puts the cart before the horse. The most important thing is to develop a body of law and a machinery of law that all nations accept and trust. To the extent that this can be achieved, history has shown that exacting compliance by force will not ordinarily be necessary. Moreover, only as this is achieved will nations lay down their arms, since the only force that can fill the vacuum created by the removal of armaments is the rule of law.

It may be asked: Is there not a third possibility—a disarmed or disarming world in which disputes are settled by the traditional techniques of diplomacy? The answer is no, because diplomacy builds upon national military strength. To the extent that security rests on diplomacy, security must also rest on armaments. The phrase "We must negotiate from strength" is the prime cliché of diplomacy.

Winston Churchill's terse way of putting it was: "We arm to parley." This maxim is well understood; but not so well understood is its negative implications for the problem of disarmament. If we arm to parley, and if "to parley" is the main way of settling international disputes, who in his right mind would propose disarming? Do we also disarm to parley?

As stressed repeatedly, there will always be a large and important range of issues for which diplomacy is the appropriate technique. Diplomacy is not something that stands in antithesis to rule of law. Rather, it is one method of conducting international affairs within a framework of law—a framework in which each kind of international dispute or relation is handled peacefully, systematically, and on the merits by the techniques best suited to it.

# PART FIVE

# *Things to Make and Do*

㉿㉿㉿㉿㉿㉿㉿㉿㉿㉿㉿㉿㉿㉿㉿㉿㉿㉿㉿㉿㉿㉿㉿

## (27)
## The Governmental Front

THIS BOOK OPENED WITH THE THEME THAT peace is not a mood or atmosphere but something that must be built. In line with that theme, it is fitting to close with a checklist of concrete activities that will help build the law structure of peace.

There are four fronts on which efforts of this kind are proceeding: the governmental front, the lawyer and bar association front, the research and university front, and the education and public opinion front. One reason why there may be some hope for progress now, where in the past there have been so much frustration and disillusionment, is the very fact that the effort is not merely that of a few lonely prophets, as in the past, but of increasingly well-organized programs on all these major fronts.

*The governmental front:* Obviously in many instances

it is governmental action which must finally put the ideas here discussed into practice.

The governmental action which has received most discussion and which is highest on the priority list of practical action is the repeal of the Connally Amendment and the depositing of a new declaration with the International Court of Justice to establish the kind of full-scale, good-faith relationship with that Court that must exist if the Court is to be effective. Similar action should be taken by every nation in the world that has not already achieved this relationship with the Court.

The debate over the Connally Amendment has occupied such a predominant place in discussion of international law in the United States that it may have tended to create the impression that this is about all there is to the job of creating international rule of law. Nothing could be further from the truth. This action, important as it is, is only the removal of a roadblock which stands in the way of many other actions which must be taken. It would be a salutary thing for the United States government and every other government to keep before it constantly a working checklist of additional tangible actions that would help advance this cause. Some of the items that might appear on such a list will be briefly noted here.

Quite apart from repeal of the Connally Amendment or the state of the declaration of any particular country, each government could administratively adopt a settled policy of making the greatest possible use of the International Court of Justice. There are many cases in which failure to take a case to the International Court, or perhaps to accept suit in the International Court, can be a matter of discretion. What is needed is not only to correct deficiencies in official declarations and institutions but also to promote a general habit and custom of applying legal procedures to legal disputes, when ordinary negotiation fails. People who have worked both with the League of Nations and with the United Nations are acutely conscious of a different attitude toward law between the two successive international organizations. Under the League system it was considered the thing to do to use courts, arbitration, advisory opinions, and other legal dispositions of essentially legal questions. The prestige of law was high. Within the United Nations, however, there seems to have grown a habit of downgrading law and minimizing its usefulness in international affairs. The inevitable symptom of this attitude is the tendency, whenever a legal consideration is involved, of referring to it not as "a matter of law" but as a "legal technicality." There is always a good name and a bad name for everything. When the law produces a result which one likes, he is apt to call it a "legal right"; when it produces a result he does not like, he is apt to call it a "legal technicality." The basic pattern of the United Nations is not at fault here, since the United Nations Charter says that legal disputes should generally be referred to the International Court of Justice. What is at fault is simply the habitual attitude and practice of individual nations, and it is clearly the duty of the nations with the strongest internal tradition of rule of law to set the pace and "change the style" by initiating and accepting resort to law in all appropriate cases.

Another important governmental action within the

immediate range of possibility for all nations is the insertion, where appropriate, in all international agreements of compromissory clauses under which the parties agree to be bound by decisions of the International Court of Justice or some other appropriate tribunal on the interpretation of the agreement. This technique has been used in hundreds of treaties and should become standard in all but two or three exceptional categories of international agreements. Indeed, it would be desirable to go even further and prepare an analysis of all existing treaties to see which ones might profitably have such a clause added by agreement where it does not now exist.

In the field of arbitration the government should examine various practical measures which could strengthen the role of arbitration on the international scene. There were two multilateral conventions formulated in 1926 and 1958 which, with various exceptions and conditions, provide for compulsory recognition of awards made in one member state when the award is up for enforcement in another member state. The United States has not joined either convention. The reason usually advanced has to do with the problem of federal-state relations which is involved in a treaty designed to require states to recognize awards of foreign origin, when in some cases they do not even recognize awards of sister states. There is good authority for supposing that this objection is not an insuperable one and could be dealt with if sufficient importance were attached to the strengthening of international arbitration that would result. Similarly, the United States might well reconsider its policy of refusal as a nation to accept arbitration with foreign nationals.

In perfecting the machinery of international justice, governments could undertake a number of improvements that have been discussed throughout this book. For example, a system of claims court in which claims between individuals and governments could be heard might be created by agreement between interested governments.

Similarly, governments could accelerate their activity in blanketing new areas of international affairs with systematic treaty law. The new draft conventions on the law of the sea and the new Antarctica Treaty are examples of this procedure, and with adequate preparation many other such areas could be handled, such as atomic energy law, the law of illegal international propaganda, possibly space law, the law of rights in international waters, and so on. Either bilateral or multilateral treaties for the encouragement and protection of international investment are also of high priority.

Another type of governmental action would be the supporting of the kind of systematic compilation, publication, and annotation of the materials of international law discussed at the beginning of the book. This is a task of such immense size and of such obvious value to governments that governmental support would be entirely appropriate.

This set of suggestions is only a partial catalog for consideration by almost any government in the world. In addition, the government of the United States and each other government could well make a specific examination of ways in which its own posture in relation to world law can be improved. Whenever such an opportunity is discovered, whether the item is a large one or a small one, the improvement should be undertaken, for it is in this way that gradually the habit and structure of law will be built. A couple of years ago, as a result of a debate in the Swiss Parliament, it came to light that the United States might be in the position of having broken a treaty with Switzerland because of an act of Congress. Under an old treaty with Switzerland the United States agreed not to draft Swiss nationals resident in the United States. The Selective Service Act was passed without, of course, taking this treaty into account. This may seem to be a small matter, but it put the United States in an uncomfortable position, particularly when it wants to take the lead in insisting on the binding force of treaties. After all, from the point of view of the other government, it is no excuse to say that the treaty violation was brought about by an act of Congress, since an act of the United States is an act of the United States whether its origin was legislative or executive. One way this situation could be cleaned up would be for the President to exercise his administrative discretion, which he is given by the Selective Service Act, to exempt Swiss nationals. In view of the number of people affected, the national security would presumably not crumble as a result. Such an action would, however, be one more demonstration that the United States is determined to take every action within its power to bolster the rule of law in its international relations.

Within the United Nations there are also tangible actions that could be taken, in addition to those already mentioned, such as officially referring legal questions to the proper legal authority, the International Court of

Justice. Much more use could be made of the advisory opinion.

Some very practical improvements could also be undertaken to facilitate the work of the International Law Commission, which is the body entrusted with the task of clarifying and codifying international law. Members of this commission are now on a part-time basis and have no funds for research or assistance. With no structural change the commission could be put on a full-time basis and given adequate financial support and research backing to help it do the enormous and complicated job which has been assigned to it.

Moreover, as Professor Louis Sohn and others have suggested, perhaps a new commission of some kind could be created which would frankly address itself to needed changes in and additions to existing international law, leaving the present commission the important but less controversial task of clarifying existing law.

# (28)
# The Legal Profession Front

THE MOMENTUM ATTAINED BY THE PEACE through law program in recent years is probably attributable more to the initiative of the American Bar Association to any other single force. The theme of peace through law has for a number of years been sounded by far-sighted lawyers and laymen. However, starting in about 1957, a rising crescendo of prominent voices was heard on this theme. A mere list of the names of some of the speeches and articles is an index of the vigor of this movement. In 1957 Dean Roscoe Pound delivered an address entitled "Toward a Law of the World." At about the same time or shortly after, may be observed the following: Henry R. Luce, "Our Great Hope: Peace is the Work of Justice"; Judge John J. Parker, "We Must Go Forward: Law in the World Community"; Charles S. Rhyne, "World Peace Through Law"; Dean Erwin N. Griswold, "Law and Peace"; Thomas E. Dewey, "A Sacred Goal: Peace Under Law"; Attorney General William P. Rogers, "International Order Under Law"; Secretary of State John Foster Dulles, "Peace Through Law"; Vice-President Richard M. Nixon, "The Rule of Law." President Eisenhower made this his theme in an address at the University of Delhi, in his speech in 1960 to the American Bar Association, and in two State of the Union messages.

The peace through law program received its great impetus when Charles S. Rhyne was president of the American Bar Association. He concentrated most of his attention and public utterances on this crusade during his year as president. He appointed a committee under Thomas E. Dewey to formulate plans on how the idea could be translated into action. This committee promptly produced an excellent report laying the groundwork for future activity. Ross Malone, who succeeded as president of the American Bar Association, appointed Rhyne chairman of a new Special Committee on World Peace Through Law, which immediately embarked on a vigorous campaign of action in the fall of 1958. The well-known international lawyer Edgar Turlington, until his untimely death, served as executive secretary of this committee and provided the committee's program with a solid foundation of research, organization, and publication.

From the beginning a considerable part of the committee's program centered around the planning of five international meetings of lawyers, four of which would be continental, and the fifth of which would be world wide. The purpose of these meetings was designed to be the launching of action programs in every country of the world, with a view to strengthening the use of law in international affairs. As a preparation for these meetings the committee first called American lawyers together in four regional meetings, with about eighty to a hundred practicing lawyers present at each, to elicit ideas on how the international meetings could be made the most productive.

Another activity of the Special Committee is the compilation of a global handbook of law and lawyers. Certainly one of the most elementary necessities for a movement of this kind is a high degree of acquaintance and understanding between the lawyers of the world. This handbook will contain not only information about the lawyers, judges, law schools, and court systems of various countries but also some basic information about the nature of their legal systems.

About one hundred affiliated Committees on Peace Through Law, under the auspices of state and local bar associations and of other organizations, have been formed and are carrying out action programs of various kinds. The compiling of material for the handbook of law and lawyers has been farmed out to state Committees on Peace Through Law, with each such committee taking two or three countries for its study. The special relationship thus created is resulting in not only correspondence but frequently in exchange visits between the two countries. As a result of all these activities, lines of systematic communication have been opened between thousands of lawyers in different countries of the world where they did not exist before.

The Special Committee has a number of activities in its program. It has made peace through law the principal theme of Law Day observances in hundreds of American communities each year. It has conducted studies of the extent to which research and teaching in international legal subjects are being conducted in American law schools. It has produced or sponsored a variety of useful publications on various aspects of international rule of law. It maintains direct ties with several thousand lawyers in different parts of the world and keeps them supplied with appropriate material.

The four regional continental meetings of lawyers are, in a sense, planning meetings for the world-wide meeting to which all countries will be invited. The global meeting will be designed to deal with a specific list of action items to be worked out by the regional planning sessions. These will not be merely meetings at which people make speeches, read papers, then go home. The intention and expectation is that out of these sessions there will emerge definite agreed lines of action, both public and private, together with a continuing provision for follow-up on a systematic basis.

# (29)
# The Research Front

IN THE PAST FEW YEARS THERE HAS BEEN a significant change in the approach to the problem of peace. This change lies in the increased realization of the part to be played by research and intellectual effort.

Both national leaders and average citizens have begun to sense that the constructing of the institutions of peace, including disarmament, dispute-settling mechanisms, economic programs, and the like, involves a staggering amount of "homework." Even if one could assume, for example, agreement in principle among nations on the desirability of a particular kind of disarmament process and system of settling disputes under law, they could not sign a workable treaty until much hard research work had been done on how this can be translated into workable plans and structures. On the scientific side, this has been recognized for some years, and intense study on the technical side has gone forward. The amount accomplished is still short of the research needed, but the groundwork has been laid. Need for similar "homework" in other fields, such as the legal and economic, is not so obvious but is equally real. For example, the problem of inspection in disarmament is crucial. Insistence on ade-

quate inspection has been one of the main themes of the
American position. Yet there are legal problems involved
on which the entire success of the American position
might depend. After all, in the United States most industry is in the hands of private owners. By what legal
right, then, does the federal government promise a
foreign government that representatives of the latter can
enter private property and make certain inspections?
This and similar questions have been investigated in the
book *Arms Control and Inspection in American Law*
(1958) by Louis Henkin. This type of problem is cited
here merely as illustrative of the vital way in which
matters of policy may be ultimately dependent on matters
of law which can only be accurately appraised as the
result of thorough research. Similarly, in the field of
economics one of the most prominent issues underlying
disarmament discussions is the question of the impact of
disarmament on the economy and on employment. This
is a subject of great complexity which is amenable to the
techniques of research and on which a substantial amount
of research has now been begun.

Throughout this book it has been evident at almost
every point that there are specific jobs of research to be
done before real progress can be made. The marshaling
of existing materials of international law is almost entirely a research job. The study of the "general principles
of law recognized by civilized nations" is a research
venture, and one of such immense proportions that it
could consume the energies of international and comparative lawyers for years. The study of new and current
facets of international law related to world peace, such as

space law, international investment law, legal problems of a disarmament treaty, atomic energy law, the law of international water rights, and so on, is an indispensable prerequisite to the making of workable treaties and other legal arrangements covering these troublesome subjects. The devising of improved machinery for international dispute-settling is a task requiring investigation of past experience and exploration of a variety of possible solutions through research. The perfection of devices to insure compliance, including the nonforce as well as the forceful measures that are or may become available, depends similarly on adequate research in the effectiveness of various devices of the past and their possible revision and adaptation to meet current needs. The obtaining of acceptance of international rule of law in any given country must begin with extensive research on the facts and the law as the basis of education both of the public and of governmental leaders. Thus, in the United States a great deal of basic research on the facts and law about the World Court, and in particular about its record of performance, has been essential to an intelligent discussion of the Connally Amendment controversy. As to the possible place of socialist legality in a scheme of world law, plainly there is room for a special kind of research effort designed to discover common elements which can be made the beginning point of some kind of working relationship. These examples are only representative of dozens of other specific lines of research that must be undertaken if the job of creating an international regime of law is to make progress. There has recently been published a volume entitled *Design for Research in International Rule of Law* (1961) which lists and discusses 113 separate research projects which are necessary to the over-all job. This volume checks off against the suggested list research now in progress or recently completed, so that the research worker can avoid duplication and can get in touch with other workers with similar interests.

The total available resources of a country like the United States for this kind of work are impressive. Research is being carried on by colleges and universities, by research centers, by foundations, by voluntary and professional associations, by business and labor organizations, by individual scholars, by both undergraduate and graduate students in the form of special papers or theses, and by government and international organization agencies. Yet, although everyone realizes that the problem of peace eclipses in importance all other problems of our times, only a tiny fraction of this colossal engine of intellectual production has been applied to the problem of peace. Perhaps the principal reason has been a failure to realize the essential role of research in building peace. The systematic publication and circulation of outlines of needed research is intended to help supply this need.

In view of the overwhelming importance of accelerated progress toward a structured peace, it would be desirable to create a systematic organizational pattern which would marshal the research resources of the United States in all fields and make the results of this research available to decision makers at the highest levels. A comprehensive organization of this kind may be thought of at three levels. First, there should be the high-level governmental agency with the specific responsibility of planning for peace and disarmament. Such an agency has been discussed under various names and at various levels from cabinet level on down. For present purposes it may be merely called the Peace Agency. It should consist of an appropriately representative group of people from the departments of government able to make a contribution to building peace. It could possibly have some nongovernmental representation, if this were felt desirable.

The next level would be a Peace Research Institute. Such an institute was organized as a nonprofit corporation in the District of Columbia in 1961, with Ambassador James J. Wadsworth as its full-time president. The purpose of the institute is to do everything a private organization can to see that research on all aspects of peace is effectively organized, to receive requests from governmental departments and ultimately the Peace Agency for needed research and to volunteer ideas and research to government agencies.

The third level, of course, consists of the operating organizations themselves—the university and other research organizations, the foundations, and so on. These are the organizations that would do the actual research work and perform the other functions necessary to the total effort.

If the total research job is to be done, the component parts of organizing that job should be identified and the necessary projects and working tools created or perfected. There are at least five identifiable functions which the Peace Research Institute should take responsibility for:

(1) providing ideas for research, (2) providing funds for research, (3) providing workers for research, (4) providing coordination for research, and (5) providing dissemination of the products of research.

As to providing ideas for research, the technique has already been established in the *Design for Research* approach. In addition to the *Design* already available in the field of international rule of law, four other comparable reports have been produced under the auspices of the Institute for International Order in the fields of science and technology, economics, communications, and decision-making. For the future the objectives should be to perfect these "designs," keep them current, and provide other "designs" for relevant areas not yet covered.

For the financing of research, the optimum solution would be to bring about the creation of a special category of peace research in which a foundation or a group of foundations would earmark a specific fund to support the projects of research listed in the various "designs for research." Thus, instead of having to make a complete case for itself afresh in every instance in competition with every other demand on foundation resources, a project within the "design for research" group would have the benefit of a strong presumption in favor of its validity. There should also be a careful coordination of public and private financing of projects, since several government departments have assets available for these purposes.

Even if one had the funds and the research ideas, they would be valueless unless competent people were motivated to undertake the research. The general neglect of topics relevant to peace has already been noted. One promising approach here would be to have each of the major professional associations organize an action committee, with a staff of its own, to maintain a year-round program of encouraging research in these areas by its members. The example of the American Bar Association Special Committee on World Peace Through Law could serve both as a prototype of what can be done and as an evidence of the results that can be achieved by this device.

The fourth function is the coordination or clearing-house function. Here again, there are two working tools already in being. One is the series of "designs for research" which, in addition to project ideas, list the current status of research on the topics mentioned. Another working tool is the publication *Current Thought on Peace and War*. This is a periodical which, among other things, reports current research on all phases of peace and war and also on recently completed work, together with a number of other useful items of information about research centers, foundations, grants, and publications. This publication, which was initiated in the winter of 1959–60, could be further enlarged to take greater account of governmental activity, research production in all the countries of the world, and other useful information. There are other related clearinghouse activities, including the American Bar Association's general list of legal research in progress, the bulletins of the State Department's Bureau of External Research in the field of international affairs, and the survey made by the Disarmament Administration of the State Department on research bearing on disarmament.

The fifth function, that of dissemination, is also ex-emplified by the periodical *Current Thought on Peace and War*. The periodical contains a fairly full digest of all published and unpublished writings in fields relevant to peace. This is intended to be a convenience to people interested in public affairs and in research, since the amount of writing is considerable and since it would be difficult for any individual to keep up with it all. More-over, much of the writing is unpublished and unavailable to the average reader. The digest calls attention to these items and makes it possible for the specialist to follow up by obtaining the unpublished material, if necessary. The Peace Research Institute should probably concern itself with seeing not only that the Peace Agency is fully supplied with the fruits of all this research and thought but also that the most effective distribution to opinion leaders and to the public is made. This leads to our final topic, the public opinion and education front.

# (30)
# Public Opinion and Education Front

AS MAJOR PUBLIC ISSUES GO, THE PEACE through law idea is a relatively novel one. People have had a century or more to become accustomed to such foreign policy issues as tariffs and reciprocal trade, mutual security, and the like. But suddenly, within a space of three or four years, they are being expected to know all about the Connally Amendment, the difference between justiciable and political issues, the difference between domestic and international issues, the nature of the International Court of Justice, and the potentialities and limitations of international law. It should not be thought surprising then if a powerful ready-made body of informed opinion does not spring up the moment controversy like that over the Connally Amendment appears.

As has been noted, through the activities of the American Bar Association and affiliated organizations a high degree of interest and enthusiasm on the peace through law program has been generated among lawyers. Perhaps the most neglected front of all now is that of general public opinion.

From the standpoint of public education the appearance of the Connally Amendment controversy is a blessing in disguise. There is nothing like a good fight to make news. If it were not for the fighting over the Connally Amendment, it is difficult to imagine how a similar amount of news, general publications, debates, editorials, and programs on the World Court and world law could have been generated. Of course, the Connally Amendment repeal was not initiated for that reason, and proponents of repeal would have been much happier if repeal could have taken place promptly with a minimum of argument. But at least widespread argument has had the valuable by-product of keeping the World Court in the news.

Specific efforts are being launched to do something
about the need for greater information activity for the
public in general. For example, there has been organized
a Committee for More Effective Use of the World Court
under the honorary chairmanship of Judge Learned
Hand, which is distributing informational material about
the World Court and particularly about the Connally
Amendment as it bears on the relations of the United
States to the World Court.

One of the most potent forces for public education in
the United States is the voluntary association. An impressive number of these associations are primarily concerned with international affairs and peace. At the same
time their officers and members must often feel a sense
of frustration when actual impact on public affairs is
measured against the amount of effort expended. Perhaps
one reason for this sense of frustration is that these associations in the past may have scattered their fire too
much. In any given year the quantum of energy they
have to expend is distributed over dozens of international issues, with the result that the impact on any single
one may not be enough to produce action. One cannot
help wondering what might be accomplished if somehow
all of these powerful organizations could arrange to concentrate for even a single year on the same international
issue. The lead for such an effort might be taken by the
Peace Research Institute, or some other organizational
avenue might be employed.

As to the role of education, if it is true—as argued
early in this book—that a new kind of world law is

needed that is somewhat different from traditional international law, it follows that there is also a need for new kinds of courses and teaching materials, both in law schools and in political science and other departments. New courses of this kind are being undertaken in a growing number of universities. It is hoped that through such efforts the coming generation of lawyers and statesmen will be armed with a concept of international law appropriate to the demands which events are certain to make on law in the years ahead.

# (31)
# Conclusion: Telescoping History

IT IS EVIDENT FROM ALL THAT HAS BEEN said that the task of building the law structure of peace is one of great difficulty and complexity. But, difficult or not, we have no choice. We must get on with the job. Jean Jacques Rousseau, in his book on education called *Emile* (1762), wrote: "The best way to teach Emile not to lean out of the window is to let him fall out. Unfortunately, the defect of this system is that the pupil may not survive to profit by his experience."

The world has been learning about international relations for centuries by a process of periodically falling out of the window. Injuries have been severe but never quite fatal. But one more fall may be our last. We must profit by our experience, for we may not be given another chance.

We have had occasion in the past to learn the lesson that tasks which for years seemed impossible of achievement have eventually yielded to hard work and patience. It was not long ago that the problem of Cyprus seemed to be one which, far from being capable of solution, merely got worse every year. The same was true of the Indus River controversy between India and Pakistan. Ingenuity, unremitting labor, a clear sense of direction, and a liberal infusion of faith and patience, all combined to elicit an eventual solution.

It is true that if we look at the monotonous way in which tensions and armaments races have led to war in the past and the way in which the best intentions for world order under law have led to disenchantment, we may take little comfort from history. But there is one factor operating now that was never present before. The shadow of the hydrogen bomb is over us all. Perhaps the mutual realization of capacity for mutual annihilation will telescope history and enable us to achieve a degree of progress in decades that in other times might have taken centuries.

There is a Brer Rabbit story which aptly sums up this theme of doing the apparently impossible. The old man was telling the little boy about the time Brer Rabbit climbed a tree. The little boy objected, "But Uncle Remus, you know rabbits can't climb trees." "Yeah, I know that," said Uncle Remus, "but Brer Fox was right behind Brer Rabbit, and Brer Rabbit was just obleeged to climb that tree."

So we too, in the presence of appalling danger, may do the apparently impossible and build the law structure of peace which many believe is now the last, best hope of earth.

# Index

## A

Abs, Dr. Herman, 173
Abuse of rights, 50
Acquired rights, 27, 49
*Ad hoc* judge, 85–86
Adjudication, 68, 101, 103
African tribal law, 30, 37, 48, 51, 52
"Alabama," 67, 194
Alfaro, Dr. Ricardo J., 79, 81, 82, 83
Alvarez, Alejandro, 150–51
American Bar Association, 19, 225, 226, 236; *MULL*, 19; Special Committee on Peace Through Law, 134, 226, 227–28, 235, 238
American self-interest, 119, 121, 123–25, 127–28
Anglo-Iranian Oil Company, 7, 75, 93, 106
Antarctica, 1959 treaty for, 57–59, 169, 223
Arbitration, 68, 95, 222
Armistice of 1949, 108, 112
Asylum case, 156
Atomic energy law, 223, 231

## B

Badawi, Dr. Abdel Hamid, 79, 81, 82, 83
Barclay, Col. Thomas, 65
Basdevant, Dr. Jules, 79, 81, 82, 83
Benedict, Ruth, 27
Benson, Egbert, 65
Bering Sea, protection of seals in, 67–68

Berlin crisis, 7, 8, 42, 103–105; Soviet claim in, 7; concerns rights of access, 7
Boundary disputes, 8, 74, 194, 206; China and India, 8; Honduras-Nicaragua, 74, 111; Sino-Indian, 109–110; Maine–Nova Scotia, 110
Bracton, Henry de, 31
Bustamente y Rivero, Dr. Jose Luis, 79, 81, 82, 83
Byzantine law, 184

## C

*Cambodia* v. *Thailand,* 166
Chagla, Mahomedali Currim, 135
Chicago *American,* editorial, 138
Chinese Code of Civil Procedure, 48
Chinese law, 31, 37, 52, 84, 152
Churchill, Winston, maxim, 217
Civic law, 31–32, 37, 41, 44, 84, 152, 167, 184
Clark, Grenville, and Louis Sohn, *World Peace Through World Law,* 77
Coded legal data, 16–21, 223; for United States Patent Office, 18; for Health Law Program, University of Pittsburgh, 18; at Western Reserve, 18; for American Bar Association, 19
Cohen, Maxwell, 16